spiralizer skinny

spiralizer skinny

Lose Weight with Easy Low-Carb Spiralizer Recipes

By Vicky Ushakova and Rami Abramov

Castle Point Books
New York

www.stmartins.com
www.castlepointbooks.com

The Castle Point Books trademark is owned by Castle Point Publications, LLC.
Castle Point books are published and distributed by St. Martin's Press.

Design: Michele L. Trombley

ISBN 978-1-250-11862-2 (trade paperback)

Our books may be purchased in bulk for promotional, educational, or business use.
Please contact your local bookseller or the Macmillan Corporate and Premium
Sales Department at 1-800-221-7945, extension 5442, or by e-mail at
MacmillanSpecialMarkets@macmillan.com.

First Edition: January 2017

10 9 8 7 6 5 4 3 2 1

CONTENTS

INTRODUCTION

Before you read any further, you should know that this isn't going to be your typical cookbook.

What's your first thought when you hear the word *diet*? Starving yourself? Bland food? Fat-free? Willpower? Something you really don't want to do?

This is a book about dieting, but not the kind you're probably thinking about. We embrace a diet in which you thrive, not one in which you starve, cut out anything with a gram of fat, lose a little weight and in a short period of time only to gain it all back. Life's too short to choose a boring, unhealthy and ineffective diet. This is a book about how to feel and look great by eating delicious food without cutting or counting calories. You'll be benefiting your health, both mental and physical.

To make everything even better, we swapped in spiralized veggies. Why? No more weighing the pros and cons before meals or hesitating before reaching for second helpings. You'll find better flavors and freshness with every meal, and more nutrients and vitamins in every dish—the list of benefits goes on. These unique recipes wouldn't be possible without spiralizing.

Just three years ago, we thought it sounded too good to be true, too. Today, millions of our blog followers eat the same way we do and are happier than they've ever been about themselves. That's because they already know what you're about to find out.

"DIETYMOLOGY"

When it comes to eating, the word diet has two meanings that are commonly used interchangeably. The original definition of *diet* means "a way of life," or in today's terms, the kinds of foods a person regularly consumes. The second, more recent definition means restricting foods and watching what you eat to reduce your weight. Due to celebrities' influence, mainstream media and this newer, popularized definition of dieting, the whole word now carries a sort of stigma. Everyone dreads starting a diet again after failing for the tenth time, right?

Therein lies the problem.

The original "way of life" meaning has a negative connotation when it should be quite the opposite. Going on a 30-day "purge" or other fad diet will only temporarily fix a permanent problem. To follow a diet for life, you must choose one that is sustainable and enjoyable.

With our book *Spiralizer Skinny*, you'll find inventive ways to transform the hassle of dieting into an adventure of delicious foods and satisfying results. What was once a burden will become second nature, and meeting all your goals (and more!) will happen with enjoyment and satisfaction.

A DIET BASED ON SCIENCE

In recent years, there has been mounting research on the health benefits of reducing dietary carbohydrates and increasing healthy fats. Additionally, an increasing number of studies are showing that a decrease in carbohydrate intake is strongly related to decreases in both type 2 diabetes and coronary heart disease (CHD).[1-3] This type of diet is called a low-carbohydrate, or low-carb, diet.

Low-carb diets are also commonly called ketogenic, or keto, diets, because when you eat fewer than 50 grams of carbohydrates per day, your body enters ketosis. Ketosis is the metabolic state in which your body primarily uses ketones (taken from dietary fat) as a source of energy instead of glucose (taken from carbs). So when you cut carbs and eat more fat, your body will start to use fat (dietary fat and stored body fat) as its main source of energy.

On a low-carb diet, you get most of your energy from fats. The few carbs you do eat come from wholesome sources like vegetables, nuts and small amounts of fruit. When eating low carb, 70 to 75 percent of the calories should come from fat, 20 to 25 percent from protein and about 5 percent from carbohydrates.

The low-carb diet has been around for a long time, although it has taken on different names and forms. You might have heard of some of these names before:

- **Atkins Diet.** This is a multiphase, low-carb diet, popularized by Robert Atkins in the late 1900s. The first two phases are very low carb.

- **LCHF Diet.** LCHF stands for low carb, high fat. It's another name for the low-carb diet.

- **Ketogenic/Ketosis/Ketone/Keto Diet.** This diet falls under the low-carb, high-fat diet but is considered stricter due to its maximum consumption of 25 grams of carbs per day to guarantee the dieter enters ketosis. The goal is to get the body to use ketones for energy and burn the most fat. Most long-term, low-carb dieters can eat up to 50 grams of carbs a day (or even more) and still maintain ketosis.

- **Banting Diet.** This diet is named after William Banting, who in 1863 wrote a booklet containing a plan for a diet that avoided most carbs. He is known for being the first to popularize a low-carb diet.

WHY EAT LOW CARB?

Today's Standard American Diet (SAD) is anything but low carb. In fact, starting in the late 1970s, when the low-fat dogma began, so did the rise of obesity, which quickly grew to an epidemic. Diabetes and heart disease skyrocketed as soon as we began increasing our carbohydrate intake, reducing our fat intake and eating chemical-laden foods. Reducing carbohydrates and opting for a more natural diet, full of fats, protein and fiber, has many health benefits, both immediate and long term.

Studies consistently show that people who eat a low-carb, high-fat diet instead of a high-carb, low-fat diet:

- Lose more weight and body fat[4-14]

- Have increased levels of "good cholesterol"[12-14]

- Show reduced blood sugar and insulin levels[15,16]

- Experience a decrease in appetite, with *less snacking and overeating*[11]

- Have consistent energy levels throughout the day

In addition, eating low carb long term has been proven to:

- Reduce blood sugar levels, because there are *no carbohydrates to break down into blood glucose*

- Reduce insulin resistance and levels, *commonly reversing and eventually ending type 2 diabetes*[15-17]

- Reduce triglycerides (fat molecules in the blood that cause heart disease)[13,14]

- Increase levels of HDL and large LDL (the good kind of cholesterol) and reduce levels of small LDL (the bad kind)[12-14]

- Significantly reduce blood pressure, leading to reduction in heart disease and stroke[18]

- Improve brain function, because *the brain runs primarily and more efficiently on ketones rather than on glucose*[19-21]

Carbohydrates: The Sugar Molecules

Carbohydrates, sugars found in food, break down in your body to create glucose. Each gram of carbohydrate eaten provides 4 calories of energy. Carbohydrate-rich foods include grains and starchy foods like wheat, flour, corn, rice, potatoes, sugar, fruits, beans and lentils.

When you eat a diet high in carbs, your body runs primarily on glucose and is in a metabolic state called glycolysis. Each time you ingest carbs, the pancreas produces insulin, a hormone that allows the glucose to get into your body's cells and use the glucose for energy. The Standard American Diet is high in carbs and causes blood sugar spikes with each meal. To combat these spikes, the pancreas produces insulin each time to break down the blood glucose.

However, the overwhelming burst of glucose-breaking insulin results in a sharp plunge in blood sugar. Have you ever had low blood sugar? You probably felt the common symptoms: irritability, faintness, headache and most likely ravenous hunger. The body starts to crave more glucose (carbs) to restore its happy, homeostatic levels by triggering the hungry feeling. The vicious cycle then repeats itself.

> **The burst of insulin results in a sharp plunge in blood sugar, triggering hunger.**

William Davis says it best in his book, *Wheat Belly*:

"Carbohydrates trigger insulin release from the pancreas, causing growth of visceral fat; visceral fat causes insulin resistance and inflammation. High blood sugars, triglycerides, and fatty acids damage the pancreas. After years of overwork, the pancreas succumbs to the thrashing it has taken from glucotoxicity, lipotoxicity, and inflammation, essentially 'burning out,' leaving a deficiency of insulin and an increase in blood glucose—diabetes."[22]

Years of constant insulin spikes multiple times a day can cause your body to develop a resistance to insulin, which can then require even more insulin to be produced in order to reduce your blood sugar as effectively as before.[2] It's very similar to alcohol tolerance, where, over time, you need to drink more to achieve the same effects. This perpetually increasing insulin resistance could lead to prediabetes, type 2 diabetes, high triglycerides, poor LDL and HDL levels, high blood pressure, high blood glucose levels and weight gain.[23]

Fats: The Energy Molecules

Fats are macronutrients that are essential for survival. Fats are utilized by our bodies for energy today and are also stored as energy for tomorrow. Each gram of fat provides about 9 calories of energy (more than twice what carbohydrates and protein provide) and is low on the glycemic index (more on that below). Foods high in fat and low in carbs will not spike your blood sugar nearly as much as high-carb foods will. Fats are the most energy-efficient form of food, which is why our bodies store any excess calories as fat for future use.

> There's no such thing as an essential carbohydrate.

A benefit of eating a lot of dietary fat is that you'll need to eat far less to feel full than if you were eating carbs. Because fat is low on the glycemic index, you won't experience the sudden "starving feeling" as you would eating a high-carb diet. Your blood sugar levels will stay consistent throughout the day and your appetite won't be at the mercy of your hormones.

On a low-carb diet, your primary source of energy is fat. Your body breaks fat down into ketones, which it then uses as a source of fuel. This metabolic state is called ketosis. Our body and brain use the ketones instead of glucose (ketones can provide up to 70 percent of the energy needed by the brain).

What most of us weren't taught in school is that our bodies can maintain stable blood sugar levels through a process called gluconeogenesis. The fats you eat and the fats stored in your body are broken down into fatty acids and glycerol. Then, through gluconeogenesis, the liver converts glycerol into glucose, keeping your blood sugar levels in a healthy and stable range.[24]

There are essential fatty acids (fats) and essential amino acids (protein); there's no such thing as an essential carbohydrate. Simply put, you do not need carbs to provide your body with glucose. Fats, protein and gluconeogenesis provide us with all the energy we need.

Bad Fats

There are some bad fats that you should avoid: processed trans fats and processed polyunsaturated fats. Processed trans fats, also known as partially hydrogenated fats, are found in processed foods, fast foods and commercially baked goods. Processed polyunsaturated fats usually come from vegetable and seed oils like soybean, canola, sunflower, safflower and corn oil.

Saturated and Monounsaturated Fats

We've all been told to avoid saturated fat because it causes cardiovascular disease. There have been many recent studies and meta studies (studies that analyze previous studies' results) by different groups of scientists trying to understand the links between cardiovascular diseases and saturated and monounsaturated fats.

In one meta study, researchers looked at 76 published studies with more than 643,000 subjects.[25] In another meta study, a different group of researchers looked at 21 studies with over 347,000 subjects.[26] Both groups of researchers came to similar conclusions after analyzing each of the data sets: eating saturated or monounsaturated fats had no effect on long-term heart disease risk.

What does this mean for us? What was previously believed to be unhealthy and dangerous for our heart health actually has no effect on it at all. Things like butter, coconut oil, animal fats and full-fat dairy products were vilified for years and blamed as the cause of our rising rates of heart disease. Today's research is proving otherwise.

The Glycemic Index

The glycemic index (GI) is a number given to a food that reflects how it affects a person's blood glucose levels. Simply put, a food with a high GI will spike a person's blood sugar more and faster than a food with a low GI. The values are based relatively on the GI value of glucose, which is 100. For example, a bowl of some popular cereals can run around 90 on the glycemic index, spiking your blood sugar first thing in the morning and sending you crashing before lunchtime rolls around.

Fats are low on the glycemic index. In fact, they barely raise blood sugar levels at all. A breakfast of full-fat yogurt, berries, eggs and even bacon will leave your blood sugar levels right where they need to be and will keep you feeling full longer. Throw some fat and fiber into the mix from nuts, seeds, or avocados and you've got a powerhouse breakfast!

The GI Scale

The GI scale, not to be confused with the glycemic index itself, places foods into three ranges: low (below 55), medium (56–69) and high (70 and above).

Even though the GI is based on accurate nutritional data, the GI scale itself is an interpretation of that data and does not need to be followed directly. There's a whole slew of foods that fall under the "low" category of the GI scale but are by no means considered low-carb or keto-friendly foods. A few examples are pasta, oats, beans and fructose.

On a low-carb diet, you should try to eat foods below 20 on the glycemic index. This excludes most carbohydrate-rich foods like pasta, oatmeal and grains. Low-glycemic and low-carb foods include meats, nuts, seeds, dairy, fats and non-starchy vegetables, such as spinach, kale, broccoli, cauliflower, asparagus and more.

The Nutritional Dark Ages

Even though we've long since surpassed the dark ages, the journey to a nutritional enlightenment has not come easily. Despite all the research and information obtained in the modern era, we still seem to be uncovering truths behind inaccurate results.

The Centers for Disease Control and Prevention's (CDC) data about obesity levels in adults in the United States ages 20 to 74 from the 1970s to 2012 reveals this truth. About 15 percent of adults were obese in 1980, and within two decades that number more than doubled. Today, about 35 percent of adults in the U.S. are obese. In 1980, 1.4 percent of U.S. adults were extremely obese and today it's nearly *five times* that amount.[27]

Why the sudden spike in obesity since the early 1980s? Something must have happened on a national scale that affected the United States as a whole.

Carbohydrates, A History

In 1977, the U.S. Senate released the *Dietary Goals for the United States*, which included a new direction for dietary guidance. In the report, carbohydrates were deemed the most crucial macronutrient of all. The U.S. Department of Agriculture (USDA) decided to use these revamped dietary goals as the basis for their new food and nutritional guide called *Hassle-Free Guide to a Better Diet*, released in 1979. This guide put fats into the same food group as sweets and alcoholic beverages—unhealthy and to be consumed in moderation. The USDA went on to use these dietary guidelines to create the *Food Guide Pyramid: A Guide to Daily Food Choices.*

The Food Guide Pyramid recommended 6 to 11 servings of the bread, cereal, rice and pasta group and 2 to 4 servings of fruit per day. Based on their guidelines for what a serving constitutes, the starchy group averages about 17.5 grams of carbs per serving and the fruits group averages about 25 grams of carbs per serving. Based on that data, the recommendation is 148.75 plus 75 grams of carbs from the two food groups, totaling nearly 225 grams of carbs per day (roughly 18 tablespoons of sugar)! Ever since the USDA released their *Dietary Guidelines* in 1980, the Surgeon General and many other government organizations have been using them as a framework for consumer nutrition education messages throughout the country.[28]

Where We Are Today

According to the American Diabetes Association (ADA), based on health data in 2012, 29.1 million people in the United States have diabetes. That's nearly 1 in 10 adults in the United States, compared to 1980, when 2.4 percent of the population had diabetes (four times fewer). It wasn't genetics' fault; diabetes became an epidemic within 30 years due to a mass dietary change.

If that number weren't staggering enough, more than 1 in 3 adults in the United States (that's 86 million people) have prediabetes, a condition in which blood sugar is constantly high and which very often leads to type 2 diabetes and a slew of other medical problems. The CDC recommends managing prediabetes and diabetes through insulin and oral medications to lower blood sugar levels rather than greatly limiting carbohydrate (sugar) intake to reduce blood sugar levels in the first place.

The CDC stresses to "eat right and be active"[30] to prevent or delay diabetes. Being mindful of eating healthy foods and trying to be more active is a good start. But what is healthy? The problem with "eating healthfully" is the open-ended nature of the phrase. What is healthy? Who can you trust to tell you what to eat? Certainly, if you accept the low-fat dogma and reduce dietary fats, then you believe you're eating healthfully. The ADA itself is encouraging people with diabetes to eat starchier, carb-filled meals and leave out full-fat products like butter, yogurt, coconut, red meats and chocolate.

The Nutritional Enlightenment

As we become more informed about nutrition, diet and our bodies through science, we are starting to understand what is truly essential and beneficial to our health. After decades of going in the wrong direction nutritionally and paying dearly for it, we are starting to discover that carbs in large quantities are more harmful than we previously thought, while most fats are actually healthy and essential.

The all-too-common symptoms of high blood sugar, bad cholesterol, insulin resistance, metabolic syndrome, type 2 diabetes and obesity are effects that can be traced back to a lifetime of high-carb diets.

The nutritional landscape is changing slowly but surely. Scientists have been conducting new research as well as reanalyzing outdated results. Fortunately, new information is much more accessible to the public today. Low-carb and similar dietary groups have been steadily growing and a nutritional revolution of sorts has already begun. It's only a matter of time before the government catches up and we'll finally see the reverse of the obesity chart from the 1980s.

2

STARTING YOUR LOW-CARB DIET

Dozens of studies have shown that switching to a low-carb diet is more effective than a high-carb, low-fat diet for weight loss and improving overall health. In addition, low-carb diets show significantly greater improvements in HDL, LDL and triglyceride levels; a greater decrease in blood pressure; and a greater insulin response than do high-carb diets.[1-18]

Most people can easily start a low-carb diet. All that's required is to reduce carbohydrates and increase fats.

THE BASICS

One of the easiest ways to cut carbs is to get rid of them! Replace carb-filled foods with alternatives that are similar in taste and texture but have far fewer carbs. That's what we've done in the recipe section of this book.

You'll find 100 recipes that are low carb, unique and delicious. The best part is that you won't need to count your calories to get results. Just eat and be happy. That's our low-carb motto.

If you're just starting out, here are a few basics that you should know:

- Freely use olive oil, avocado oil, coconut oil or butter when you cook.

- Eat fatty and protein-rich foods like eggs, bacon and avocados for breakfast. You can find more low-carb breakfast recipes at www.tasteaholics.com/breakfast.

- Drink plenty of water. Coffee and tea are great options, too. Use a splash of heavy cream instead of milk or creamer in your coffee.

DIABETES? CONSULT WITH YOUR DOCTOR

If you have diabetes, a low-carb diet can still work for you. It can begin to reverse type 2 diabetes and strongly improve blood sugar control in type 1 diabetes. If you take medication (insulin) for your diabetes, you may have to immediately decrease your doses.

You should consult with your doctor before starting a low-carb diet. Your doctor may recommend a trial period where you eat fewer carbs per day while under a health practitioner's supervision to monitor your blood glucose and insulin doses. For type 1 diabetes, you should always eat above 50 grams of carbohydrates a day to prevent ketoacidosis (a condition that differs from ketosis).

- Replace common sides like pasta, potatoes and rice with some of our sides or any salads you enjoy.

- Avoid bread, desserts, sugar and other high-carb foods.

WHAT'S LOW CARB AND WHAT'S NOT

Low-carb success is easy when you know what to look for and what to avoid. Use this list as a quick reference and shopping list if you're just starting out. Once you've been eating low carb for a little while, you'll get accustomed to it and you'll become more creative as you discover a new world of interesting and delicious foods (that are actually *good* for you!).

The Good

HEALTHY FATS AND OILS	Coconut oil, butter, lard and bacon fat, olive oil, avocados, fish oil, nuts and seeds.
MEATS	Chicken, beef, lamb, pork, venison and others. *Grass-fed and organic are the healthiest.*
FISH AND SEAFOOD	Salmon, cod, shrimp, octopus, tuna, tilapia, bass and others. *Wild-caught is the healthiest.*
NONSTARCHY VEGETABLES AND LEAFY GREENS	Spinach, kale, Swiss chard, broccoli, mushrooms, cucumbers, cherry tomatoes, zucchini, yellow squash, spaghetti squash and others. *Most leafy, green vegetables are very low in carbs.*
EGGS	*Whole, organic, pasture-raised are best.*
FULL-FAT DAIRY	Cheeses, unsweetened almond milk, heavy cream, yogurt and butter. *Any dairy low in carbs and high in saturated and/or monounsaturated fat is generally good.*
NUTS AND SEEDS (IN SMALL AMOUNTS)	Almonds, walnuts, macadamia nuts, cashews, pecans, sunflower seeds, pumpkin seeds, flaxseeds and chia seeds.
BERRIES AND FRUITS (IN SMALL AMOUNTS)	Blueberries, raspberries, blackberries, strawberries, currants, avocados, olives, lemons and limes.
SWEETENERS AND SUGAR ALCOHOLS	Erythritol, stevia, Truvia and xylitol. *Sugar alcohols listed on nutritional labels do not count toward your carb limit, so you can subtract them from the total carbs listed just as you would fiber. Be careful, though, because some can cause a laxative effect in large quantities.*
UNSWEETENED BEVERAGES	Water, coffee, tea, fresh-squeezed vegetable juices, carbonated water (club soda) and erythritol/stevia-sweetened beverages.

GRAINS AND STARCHY FOODS	Bread, cereal, bagels, pasta, rice, potatoes, corn, cornstarch, wheat, rice, barley, oats and quinoa.
LEGUMES	Beans, peas and lentils.
SUGARY FOODS AND DRINKS	Fountain drinks, chocolate milk, fruit juices, desserts, milk chocolate, pastries, candy bars, etc.
PROCESSED POLYUNSATURATED FATS	Vegetable and most seed oils, including canola, soybean, corn, grapeseed, peanut and sunflower oil.
PROCESSED TRANS FATS	Avoid processed foods, fast foods, margarine and commercially baked goods.

What's Low Carb *Enough*

We're all human and we all need a break sometimes. There are many diets that will have you believe losing weight or being healthy is black and white, but there's always some gray if you make room for it. Knowing which foods are naturally low-carb friendly or how to *make* them more low-carb friendly is key.

A perfect example of a low-carb friendly dessert is chocolate. Not the kind you'll find on your way to the cashier; we're talking about the good stuff. Real dark chocolate with all its natural nuances is high in fat, fiber and antioxidants. Look for a brand without preservatives or emulsifiers and a bar that's 85 percent cocoa or higher.

Here are a few other food and drink items that will come in handy for keeping you on track at the beginning of your low-carb diet.

SWEETS AND DESSERTS	Dark chocolate, cocoa nibs, peanut and other nut butters, sugar-free Jell-O, whipped cream and sugar-free desserts (take a look at our dessert recipes on www.tasteaholics.com/desserts).
ALCOHOL	Clear liquors (vodka, tequila, whiskey, etc.), dry red and white wines and light beers (see more options on www.tasteaholics.com/alcohol).

As with all foods, check the nutrition label and ingredients; if sugar is listed, it best be in very low quantities.

WHAT TO EXPECT WHEN STARTING YOUR LOW-CARB DIET

Instant Weight Loss

It's a common occurrence within the first week of starting a low-carb diet to lose a significant amount of weight. The weight loss could range greatly, anywhere from 3 to 15 pounds.

Don't be alarmed (or too excited)! It's not fat loss just yet. This is completely normal and is mostly water weight.

This sudden water weight loss happens often. When you reduce carbohydrates in your diet, your body burns through the rest of your glycogen stores. Each gram of glycogen binds to 3 or 4 grams of water. When those glycogen stores are depleted, the water flushes away. It's a great boost in the beginning, but it is not permanent. That's why when you see this weight fall off you, don't stop!

During the first week of eating low carb, you start burning the fat you eat for energy as well as the excess fat your body has stored. It's typical to lose anywhere between 3 and 8 pounds of fat within the first month without eating at a caloric deficit at all. Just eat low-carb, high-fat meals until you're satisfied and you'll still shed pounds.

You can, of course, eat at a deficit to accelerate the fat-loss process. An added benefit of eating low carb is your body will tap into your fat stores more efficiently because it's already used to burning fat for energy, unlike when you eat high carb.

The Keto Flu

When the body has been addicted to carbs for a long time, removing those carbs can cause it to go through a form of withdrawal. This withdrawal is commonly called the keto flu. This generally happens in the first week or two of starting the low-carb diet, but it can also occur any time your nutrition is neglected. The symptoms you may experience are similar to those that occur when you have the flu virus and may include:

- Fatigue

- Headaches

- Cough

- Sniffles

- Irritability

- Nausea

> The keto flu phase means your body is readjusting to using fat as its primary source of energy.

It's important to know that this is not the real influenza virus. It's called keto flu due to the similar symptoms people experience, but it is not contagious and does not involve an actual virus.

Many people who experience these symptoms believe the diet caused them to get sick and immediately go back to eating carbs. On the contrary, going into the keto flu phase actually means your body is readjusting to using fat as its primary source of energy.

One of the main causes of keto flu is the lack of electrolytes, especially sodium, in your body. Processed foods have a lot of added sodium. When starting a new, better way of eating, people cut out a lot of processed foods and start eating whole, natural foods instead. Overall, it's a great change, but this causes a sudden drop in sodium intake.

In addition to reducing sodium intake, your body stops storing as much sodium as it did before. Remember insulin? It tells your kidneys to store sodium. Reducing your carb intake reduces your insulin levels, which in turn tells your kidneys to release excess sodium.[31] If you notice yourself going to the bathroom more on a low-carb diet, you're not crazy—excess water is being flushed out by your excretory system.

Collectively, between your reduced sodium intake and your kidneys flushing excess sodium, you are very low on sodium and other electrolytes.

Alleviating the Keto Flu

The best way to alleviate the keto flu is to add more sodium to your diet. We found these to be our favorite ways of getting more sodium:

- Adding more salt to your food

- Drinking soup broth

- Eating plenty of salty foods like bacon and pickled vegetables

If you don't feel better immediately, just remember that the keto flu will go away within a few days and you'll come out a fat-burning machine!

SUCCEEDING IN YOUR LOW-CARB DIET

What seems like instant success actually comes gradually. Taking control of your diet and your health will always have ups and downs, and that's absolutely normal. Here are some tips to bring you closer to success and keep you anchored even when things aren't looking up.

Don't Limit Yourself

Eating a low-carb diet does not mean that food has to taste bad. It's that simple. We've been eating more deliciously than ever before. Don't believe us? Check out www.tasteaholics.com/recipes, and you'll be amazed at how good "health food" can really taste. Creating low-carb recipes has challenged us creatively and expanded our tastes beyond the Standard American Diet.

You might be thinking: "Well, I don't have time to come up with recipes like you." Why should you? That's why this cookbook and blogs like ours exist! In addition to recipes, you can find helpful low-carb meal plans at www.tasteaholics.com/meal-plans/.

Forget Starving

We live in a world that recommends malnutrition to lose weight and "get healthy." It's a major misconception that you have to starve yourself to see results. This is simply not true and actually damaging to your long-term health. You can hit your goals without damaging your body in the process.

Every body has its own needs. You should know what you need to be eating. These needs are based on:

- Your current lean body weight (total body weight minus body fat)

- Daily activity levels (do you sit behind a desk all day, wait tables, play professional sports?)

- Whether or not you work out. If so:

  - The types of workouts (weight lifting, running or both)
  - Hours per week of each type

- Gender

- Age

- Your goal:

  - Lose weight
  - Maintain weight
  - Gain muscle

To simplify this whole process, we created an easy calculator you can use any time on our site. Visit www.tasteaholics.com/calculator and you'll be able to plug in your information as well as estimate what your body fat percentage is if you don't already know it. You'll get an idea of how many calories you should try to eat every day as well as a breakdown in macronutrients (fat, protein and carbohydrates) if you want to get a bit more technical.

If you decide to track what you eat, we recommend food-tracking apps such as MyFitnessPal. They make tracking easy: you simply enter your meal ingredients individually and it will automatically calculate all of the data for you. It's a great way to speed your progress and give you a visual reminder to stay on track.

Track Progress the Right Way

Stepping on a scale in the morning and hoping to see a difference is one of the least accurate ways to track progress. Our bodies don't work that way. Many factors contribute to weight, causing it to fluctuate not just daily but hourly. Don't rely on numbers alone!

There are a few more reliable ways to track progress, and they take no longer than a minute per week.

1. The first method is using a tape measure. Take a measurement of your waist once a week and track your progress that way. Try to pick the morning of the same day during the week and stick to it for consistency. Set an alarm in your calendar to remind you and write the measurement down so you can follow your progress easily.

2. The second method, which is our preferred method, is to simply take pictures once a week or every two weeks. Over time, you'll see a huge difference. Focus on the long term and remember: progress is slow and steady.

It's absolutely critical to track progress because it shows you just how well you're doing and acts as an anchor if you're having any doubts. Best of all, it'll motivate you to succeed even further!

It's a Lifestyle Change

A huge misconception about eating low carb is that it's a diet. To some people, that's all it is, and it's very likely that they are the ones who won't succeed. Eating low carb means your diet regularly consists of foods low in carbs and high in fat and protein. You're not on a diet—it's your diet and your way of life.

Today, being "on a diet" actually means you are eating fewer calories every day than your body uses. Your body is forced to burn energy it has stored in your fat and muscles. It would cause less confusion if we changed "I'm on a diet" to "I'm in a deficit."

One of the best things about eating low carb is that you don't need to eat less food or fewer calories. In fact, it is recommended you eat until you feel full and satisfied. The beauty of eating low carb is that you still get to eat delicious food that isn't pumped full of chemicals in an effort to make it taste better.

Lead by Example

We've all got people around us who will doubt and oppose what we do, regardless of what it is. It will be no different with this diet, and we can't blame them. After all, most of us have been taught throughout our lives that fat is bad and carbs are good.

We found the best way to leave the doubters in the dust is to lead by example. Losing weight, having more energy, and feeling and looking better every day makes you more confident and radiant. If you take charge of your health and stand up for the truth, those doubters just might become curious about this way of life you've begun!

3

AN INTRODUCTION TO SPIRALIZING
AND OUR RECIPES

By this point, you may be thinking, "What does spiralizing have to do with eating low carb?"

Spiralizers have gained popularity over the last few years thanks to their simple design and vast health benefits. At first glance, a spiralizer simply transforms a few basic vegetables (and fruits) into noodles. The real benefits, however, come from incorporating spiralized vegetables into your diet daily and creatively. When you let your imagination run wild with a spiralizer, you'll find yourself eating more vegetables, consuming fewer calories and carbohydrates and even saving time in the kitchen.

When starting out on a low-carb diet, you have to cut out lots of foods you probably love. One of the most beloved carbs in America is pasta. People have a hard time giving up spaghetti, macaroni, fettuccine and all the other pasta family members. That's where the spiralizer comes in!

BENEFITS OF SPIRALIZING

A Side-by-Side Analysis

Zucchini is one of the most popular vegetables to spiralize because of its strong resemblance in look and texture to traditional spaghetti when spiralized. The difference between the two nutritionally will surprise you! One medium zucchini yields roughly the same amount of "noodles" as a cup of spaghetti. The zucchini noodles (zoodles) have about 33 calories and 5 net carbs (total carbs minus fiber). A cup of spaghetti is about 220 calories and 40 net carbs. Zoodles take 3 minutes to cook while spaghetti can take around 15. See the comparison table below:

INGREDIENT	1 MEDIUM ZUCCHINI	1 CUP SPAGHETTI
Calories	33	220
Net Carbs	5	40
Cook Time (in minutes)	3	15

Beyond the ease and convenience of a quickly spiralized zucchini, you'd also be eating a more nutrient-dense meal. One medium zucchini has more than half of your daily vitamin C needs! It's also a good source of antioxidants, potassium, folate and vitamin A.

That's just zucchini; think of all the other delicious, colorful, healthy vegetables you can incorporate into your diet with this one easy technique.

Retain Flavor and Texture

The texture and consistency of spiralized vegetables strongly resembles pasta. Since flavors primarily come from the sauces and spices added to the dish, switching out an ingredient like spaghetti for zoodles is easy and very forgiving.

When we first tried our Chicken Squash Alfredo recipe with yellow squash noodles, we couldn't believe how similar it felt and tasted to traditional spaghetti. The best part was being able to enjoy a second serving knowing yellow squash is a low-calorie, low-carb, gluten-free and grain-free choice!

Increase Vegetable Consumption

Years of phony fad diets and incorrect scientific test results have come and gone. The thing that remains ingrained in our minds is "eat more vegetables," and for good reason! Vegetables are an incredibly diverse group that yields flavorful and nutrient-dense foods.

Eating more veggies is beneficial to everyone, regardless of age, background or wellness. Considering today's Standard American Diet (SAD), everybody could use more vitamins, minerals and fiber. Dietary fiber is especially important for your metabolism and digestion (plus it helps keep you full longer).

Switching out high-carb foods like pasta for low-carb vegetables is particularly beneficial in terms of health and wellness. The SAD is higher in carbs than ever before. The tired dogma of consuming foods low in fat as being healthy is slowly fading away. Science is embracing natural, full-fat foods as beneficial while recognizing processed, low-fat foods as being detrimental to health. Besides, what's healthy about a fat-free, artificially flavored muffin that'll send your blood sugar soaring, only to quickly drop and make you crave another?

Lowering your carbs by eliminating processed and unnatural foods in lieu of nutrient-dense veggies will help you feel fuller, less bloated and more energized throughout your day.

Faster Meal Preparation

Who has extra time to spare for cooking these days? Spiralizers can help reduce overall time spent in the kitchen. Spiralizing a vegetable increases the surface area by cutting it into dozens of noodles, reducing the cook time significantly. Sometimes you don't even need to cook the noodles, as many of the veggies can be eaten raw! This means less time spent cooking and more nutrients preserved: it's a win-win.

SPIRALIZING BASICS

The Spiralizer

Purchasing a quality spiralizer will ensure that each vegetable is spiralized in seconds, making perfect noodles without hassle. The cleanup is quick and storing it is effortless!

We purchased the Veggetti Pro Tabletop Spiral Vegetable Cutter, which comes with three blade attachments for thin noodles, thick noodles and ribbons. The ribbon attachment is particularly handy when you need to quickly shred cabbage or cut onions. The Veggetti quickly suctions to your countertop and stays in place while you spiralize your fruits and vegetables. It truly makes spiralizing simple.

The blades are dishwasher safe and the entire thing can be rinsed off and dried in seconds. It also disassembles quickly for easy storage, even in the smallest of kitchens. For an even more compact and portable option, you can purchase the handheld Veggetti Spiral Vegetable Cutter. Think of it as a pencil sharpener for vegetables, but what comes out is noodles! The handheld Veggetti isn't able to spiralize vegetables into ribbons, however.

Whichever spiralizer you get, you'll love the results, especially paired with our delicious recipes!

1. First, choose the right kind of vegetable. You want to choose something at least 2 inches in diameter and one that is relatively straight. For example, many yellow squash can be curved at one end; try to pick one that is straight from tip to tip. The vegetable shouldn't be hollow, as a pepper would be, but firm and whole throughout, like a zucchini.

2. Once you have your vegetable rinsed and clean, trim the ends off of each side to create a flat surface. The cut should be perpendicular to your cutting board or countertop.

3. Prepare your work surface by ensuring the countertop is clean and dry. Secure the spiralizer to the countertop. Our spiralizer suctions to the surface by switching the handle from "off" to "on." Place a bowl by the blade end of the spiralizer into which to spiralize the vegetable.

4. Select your blade and insert it into the spiralizer. Move the arm back to make room for your vegetable and attach it onto the spikes securely. Press the vegetable gently to ensure it is firmly attached to both the spikes and your selected blade attachment.

5. Begin turning the crank on the spiralizer while pushing gently with the other hand on the slider. The vegetable should begin to emerge as noodles or ribbons into the bowl you placed by the blade attachment.

Spiralizer-Friendly Foods

The lists below include low-carb foods that can be spiralized and how to prepare them for spiralizing.

ITEM	PREPARATION NEEDED FOR SPIRALIZING
Apple	Remove the stem.
Beet	Cut the ends off and peel.
Broccoli (stem)	Cut the ends off and peel.
Butternut Squash	Cut off the bulbous half. Cut the end of the straighter half off and peel its hard skin multiple times until you reach the bright orange inside.
Cabbage	No prep is needed.
Carrot	Cut the ends off and peel.
Celeriac	Cut the ends off and peel completely.
Chayote	Cut the ends off.
Cucumber	Cut the ends off. Peeling is optional.
Daikon Radish	Cut the ends off and peel.
Jicama	Cut the ends off and carefully slice the waxy skin off.
Parsnip	Cut the ends off and peel.
Pear	Remove the stem.
Rutabaga	Cut the ends off.
Yellow Squash	Cut the ends off. Peeling is optional.
Zucchini	Cut the ends off. Peeling is optional.

ABOUT THE RECIPES

In the next section of this book, you'll find 100 delicious, spiralized recipes, all of which are low carb. We created and tested most of these recipes throughout the last two years, with many of them serving as staples in our daily diet. Some are simple, others are more challenging, but all of them can be made at home with the help of your spiralizer.

Our hope is that you'll be left with a deeper understanding of your body's needs and gain a multitude of go-to recipes that will help kick-start you into a healthier lifestyle.

Recipe Notes

We wrote the following recipe notes to hopefully clear up any confusion or questions that may arise throughout the course of the book. Feel free to refer back to this section if you need to, or read through it in the beginning to keep in mind.

CHICKEN	In all of our recipes, we use boneless, skinless chicken breasts and boneless, skinless chicken thighs. Feel free to use skin-on (the skin has plenty of good fats)! If you have bone-in chicken thighs, be sure to debone them before preparing the recipe. If you like, you can swap out chicken breasts for chicken thighs and vice versa.
BEEF	We usually use 85 percent lean ground beef, unless otherwise stated. If you have a different percentage leanness on hand, go ahead and use that. We prefer 85 percent lean ground beef because the fattier, the merrier! It's affordable and delicious and gives a good juiciness to the recipes.
SOY SAUCE	If you're gluten-free, be sure to find a gluten-free soy sauce. Soy sauce is made from soybeans and wheat, but some gluten-free soy sauces are instead made from rice.
BROTH	We most commonly use chicken broth for the recipes that require it. Other common broths include beef, vegetable and seafood. In our recipes, we specify the broth if we think it will affect the flavor or is important for the results. If you see just "broth" listed, feel free to use your favorite broth. Swapping vegetable broth and leaving out any meats in a soup to create a vegetarian version is also fine.
SALT	It is important to note the difference between table salt and sea salt. Table salt is very fine, while sea salt is coarse and flaky. We use sea salt in all of our recipes. If you only have table salt, you will need to reduce the amount you use in each recipe because only table salt is more densely compacted in measuring spoons. Always salt a bit and give your food a taste before adding more.
PEELING VEGETABLES	Feel free to peel any vegetables if you don't want to eat their skins. We specify which vegetables we peel (e.g., carrots and butternut squash).

SOUPS AND SALADS

SPICY COCONUT THAI SOUP

A little heat never hurt anybody! Featuring sweet, soothing coconut milk and delicate mushrooms, this Spicy Coconut Thai Soup is the perfect meatless dinner option that still delivers tons of flavor.

PREP TIME: **20 minutes**
COOK TIME: **18 minutes**
SERVES: **4–6 people**

INGREDIENTS:

2 tablespoons olive oil

1-inch cube ginger, grated

1 stalk lemongrass

2 tablespoons red pepper flakes

1 (15-ounce) can coconut milk

1 quart chicken or vegetable broth

12 ounces mushrooms, sliced

¼ cup chopped cilantro

Juice of 1 lime

Salt and pepper

INSTRUCTIONS:

1. Heat the olive oil in a large soup pot over medium heat, add the grated ginger, lemongrass stalk and red pepper flakes and cook for 2 minutes to release their flavors.

2. Shake the can of coconut milk well so that it's fully incorporated. Add the coconut milk and broth to the pot.

3. Let the soup come to a boil and then lower the heat to a simmer.

4. Add the sliced mushrooms and cook for about 10 minutes.

5. Add the chopped cilantro and lime juice, season with salt and pepper and serve.

CHICKEN ZOODLE SOUP

Revisit this classic soup with your spiralizer and it will be low carb and even healthier! There's nothing better than our Chicken Zoodle Soup for the cold winter months, especially if you're fighting off a cold.

PREP TIME: 15 minutes
COOK TIME: 45 minutes
SERVES: 4–6 people

INGREDIENTS:

2 tablespoons olive oil

1 white onion, chopped

4 cloves garlic, chopped

1-inch cube ginger, minced

2 medium carrots, chopped

2 stalks celery, chopped

2 teaspoons salt

½ teaspoon black pepper

1 tablespoon dried basil

1 tablespoon dried oregano

½ teaspoon ground turmeric

1 quart chicken broth

2 cups water

10 ounces boneless, skinless chicken thighs

4 bay leaves

2 large zucchini

INSTRUCTIONS:

1. In a large soup pot, heat the olive oil over medium heat. Add the chopped onion, garlic and ginger and cook until the onion becomes translucent and the garlic is fragrant, 4 to 5 minutes.

2. Add the carrots and celery to the pot. Add the salt, pepper, basil, oregano and turmeric and stir to combine.

3. Add the chicken broth and water, increase the heat and bring the mixture to a boil.

4. Lower the heat to a simmer, add the chicken thighs and bay leaves and cook for 30 minutes.

5. Remove the cooked chicken thighs from the soup with tongs, shred them using two forks and add them back into the soup. Cook for 15 minutes longer.

6. Trim the ends off the zucchini and spiralize them into thin noodles. Add the noodles to the soup pot during the last 2 or 3 minutes of cooking. Remove the bay leaves and serve.

CHICKEN SOUP

CHICKEN SOUP

1 Small Chicken
3-4 pints Water
Salt & Pepper
Fresh Herbs

1 Onion
1 Bay Leaf
1 blade Mace

ROSEMARY CHICKEN PARSNIP SOUP

Fresh rosemary is the secret to the mouthwatering flavors of our Rosemary Chicken Parsnip Soup. It is light yet hearty and makes a great meal for supper.

PREP TIME: **10 minutes**
COOK TIME: **55 minutes**
SERVES: **4–6 people**

INGREDIENTS:

12 ounces boneless, skinless chicken breasts

2 tablespoons olive oil

8 ounces white mushrooms, diced

1 large white onion, diced

1 quart chicken broth

1 sprig fresh rosemary

Salt and pepper

2 cups water

2 large parsnips

INSTRUCTIONS:

1. On a clean work surface, using a meat tenderizer or rolling pin, pound the chicken breasts until they are about ½ inch thick.

2. Heat 1 tablespoon of the oil in a large skillet over medium heat and fry the breasts for 5 to 7 minutes on each side or until golden on the outside and the juices run clear when cut.

3. Meanwhile, heat the remaining 1 tablespoon of oil in a medium pan, add the diced mushrooms and onion and sauté over medium heat for about 5 minutes, until the onions become translucent.

4. Transfer the mushrooms and onions to a large soup pot set over medium heat.

5. Pour some chicken broth into the pan you sautéed the vegetables in and use a wooden spoon to help scrape off all the caramelized bits. Pour everything from the pan into the pot as well.

6. Once the chicken breasts are fully cooked, remove them from the pan and shred them with two forks.

7. Add the shredded chicken, rosemary, salt and pepper to taste, water and the rest of the chicken broth to the pot.

8. Trim the ends off the parsnips, peel them and spiralize them into thick noodles. Add them to the pot as well.

9. Allow the soup to come to a gentle boil, reduce the heat to low and simmer for 30 to 40 minutes. Remove the rosemary sprig and serve.

CABBAGE TOMATO SOUP

If you enjoy a delicious, hearty meal, you'll love this Cabbage Tomato Soup.
It's full of tons of nutrients and flavors, making it a great meal,
especially if you're feeling a little under the weather.

PREP TIME: 15 minutes
COOK TIME: 45 minutes
SERVES: 6–8 people

INGREDIENTS:

1 head green cabbage

2 large carrots

2 medium yellow onions,
    chopped

4 Roma tomatoes, chopped

4 cloves garlic, chopped

2 green bell peppers,
    chopped

2 cups tomato juice

1 quart beef broth

1 quart water

Salt and pepper

Fresh parsley, for garnish

INSTRUCTIONS:

1. Using the ribbon attachment on your spiralizer, shred the head of cabbage.

2. Trim the ends off the carrots, peel them and spiralize them into thick noodles.

3. Add all the ingredients, except the parsley, to a large pot and let the soup simmer for about 45 minutes.

4. Garnish with the fresh parsley and serve warm.

LEMON DIJON CHICKEN SOUP

Lemon Dijon Chicken Soup is hearty yet fresh, with the tangy flavors of lemon and Dijon mustard. When you're craving soup in the summer, this is the one for you! It's low carb and highly nutritious, with veggies in abundance but no extra calories from carb-y noodles.

PREP TIME: 35 minutes
COOK TIME: 15 minutes
SERVES: 4–6 people

INGREDIENTS:

2 large carrots

1 large zucchini

1 tablespoon Dijon mustard

Juice of 2 lemons

1 pound boneless, skinless chicken thighs

2 tablespoons olive oil

1 onion, chopped

1 quart chicken broth

2 cups water

5 ounces fresh kale

½ cup sour cream

INSTRUCTIONS:

1. Trim the ends off the carrots and peel them. Spiralize them into thin or thick noodles according to your preference.

2. Trim the ends off the zucchini and spiralize into thin or thick noodles according to your preference.

3. In a deep mixing bowl, combine the two types of noodles using tongs to toss them.

4. Dress the noodles with the Dijon mustard and the lemon juice. Let the noodles sit for 30 minutes.

5. Meanwhile, dice the chicken thighs into bite-size pieces.

6. Heat the olive oil in a soup pot over medium heat, add the chopped onion and cook until the onion is translucent, about 5 minutes.

7. Add the chicken broth and water to the soup pot and bring it to a boil. Add the diced chicken thighs and kale and lower the heat to a simmer. Cook for 15 minutes.

8. Add the sour cream and noodles (and the residual mustard and lemon juice from the bowl) to the pot and let simmer for 20 more minutes before serving.

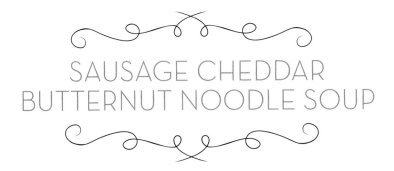

SAUSAGE CHEDDAR BUTTERNUT NOODLE SOUP

An amazing fall soup that's filling and delicious, Sausage Cheddar Butternut Noodle Soup has a creaminess that's perfect for cold weather. You can add more or less chicken broth to make the soup your preferred thickness.

PREP TIME: 20 minutes
COOK TIME: 1 hour
SERVES: 4–6 people

INGREDIENTS:

4 tablespoons olive oil

2 yellow onions, diced

8 cloves garlic, minced

1 quart chicken broth

1 quart water

4 (2-ounce) sausage links

2 large butternut squash

½ teaspoon ground turmeric

1 teaspoon paprika

1 teaspoon garlic powder

2 teaspoons dried oregano

Salt and pepper

12 ounces sharp cheddar cheese, shredded

INSTRUCTIONS:

1. Heat 2 tablespoons of the olive oil in a large soup pot over medium heat. Add the onions and garlic to the pot and cook until translucent, about 5 minutes.

2. Add the chicken broth and water, bring the soup to a boil and then lower the heat to a simmer.

3. Add the remaining 2 tablespoons of olive oil to a medium pan over medium heat and fry the sausage links on each side for 2 minutes, until they are browned all around.

4. Remove the sausages from the pan and slice them into ¾-inch slices. Add the sausage slices back to the pan and cook for another 3 minutes, until they're almost fully cooked, and then add them to the simmering soup pot.

5. Cut off the bulbous half from the butternut squash. Cut off the end of the straighter half and peel its hard skin multiple times until you reach the bright orange inside. Spiralize the butternut squash into thick noodles and add them to the soup.

6. Add the turmeric, paprika, garlic powder, oregano and salt and pepper to taste and continue to simmer for 30 minutes.

7. Lastly, add the shredded cheddar cheese and allow it to melt in the soup. Cook the soup for an additional 15 minutes and serve.

EGG DROP SOUP

Egg Drop Soup is one of our favorite dishes when we eat at Chinese restaurants.
Simplicity is the key to this delicious Asian classic.

PREP TIME: 10 minutes
COOK TIME: 20 minutes
SERVES: 4–6 people

INGREDIENTS:

½ head green cabbage

2 medium carrots

1 quart chicken broth

2 scallions, thinly sliced

Salt and pepper

4 large eggs

INSTRUCTIONS:

1. Using the ribbon attachment on your spiralizer, shred the cabbage.

2. Trim the ends off the carrots, peel them and spiralize them into thick noodles.

3. Heat the chicken broth in a pot over medium-high heat. Add the shredded cabbage, carrot noodles, scallion and salt and pepper to taste, and bring the soup to a boil.

4. Beat the eggs in a bowl. While stirring the soup, drop in a spoonful of the eggs at a time, stirring continuously to prevent clumping.

5. Allow the soup to cook for another 5 minutes and serve.

SAUSAGE MINESTRONE SOUP
WITH BROCCOLI RIBBONS

The classic minestrone flavor with the addition of sweet Italian sausage and spiralized broccoli makes this Sausage Minestrone Soup with Broccoli Ribbons burst with savory flavors.

PREP TIME: 15 minutes
COOK TIME: 40 minutes
SERVES: 4–6 people

INGREDIENTS:

2 tablespoons olive oil

8 ounces sweet Italian sausage, casings removed

1 medium white onion, diced

2 celery stalks, chopped

1 14.5 ounce can whole tomatoes, drained and chopped

2 medium carrots

2 broccoli stems

1 quart chicken broth

2 cups water

1 head green cabbage

¼ teaspoon red pepper flakes

¼ teaspoon dried rosemary

Salt and pepper

Grated Parmesan, for garnish

INSTRUCTIONS:

1. Heat the olive oil in a large soup pot over medium heat, add the sausage and cook until it's browned and crumbled, which should take about 5-8 minutes.

2. Remove the sausage from the pot and transfer to a bowl, then add the onion to the pot and cook until translucent, about 5 minutes.

3. Add the chopped celery and canned tomatoes and stir to combine.

4. Trim the ends off the carrots and broccoli stems and peel them lightly. Spiralize them both into ribbons and add to the soup pot.

5. Add the chicken broth and water, bring the soup to a boil and then lower the heat to a simmer.

6. Shred the green cabbage using the ribbon attachment on the spiralizer and add it to the simmering soup pot.

7. Add the sausage back to the pot.

8. Season the soup with the red pepper flakes, rosemary and salt and pepper to taste. Stir everything well to combine and let the soup simmer for about 20 minutes.

9. Garnish each portion with freshly grated Parmesan cheese and serve.

LEMON-PEPPER SALMON AND PARSNIP NOODLE SOUP

Lemon and pepper always go great with salmon and even better in soup form.
Lemon-Pepper Salmon and Parsnip Noodle Soup is a delicious chowder with
a citrusy kick you'll enjoy any time of the year.

PREP TIME: 10 minutes
COOK TIME: 25 minutes
SERVES: 4 people

INGREDIENTS:

1 pound fresh salmon fillet

Salt and cracked black
    pepper

3 tablespoons olive oil

1 white onion, diced

4 cloves garlic, minced

4 medium parsnips

2 cups vegetable broth

2 cups water

Juice of 2 lemons

salt to taste

1 teaspoon pepper

1 teaspoon dried basil

½ teaspoon red pepper
    flakes (optional)

INSTRUCTIONS:

1. Season the salmon fillet with salt and pepper.

2. Heat 1 tablespoon of the olive oil in a large skillet over
   medium heat, add the salmon and fry for 5 to 7 minutes on
   each side or until it's pale and flakes easily with a fork.

3. Meanwhile, heat the remaining 2 tablespoons of olive oil in
   a soup pot over medium heat, add the onion and garlic and
   sauté until the onion is translucent, about 5 minutes.

4. Trim the ends off the parsnips, peel them, spiralize them into
   thick noodles and add them to the soup pot. Toss the noodles
   to coat them in the olive oil and cook for about 2 minutes.

5. Add the vegetable broth, water, lemon juice, salt to taste, 1
   teaspoon pepper, dried basil and red pepper flakes. Stir to
   combine and bring the soup to a boil, then reduce the heat
   and let it simmer for 10 minutes.

6. Shred the cooked salmon with a fork and add it to the
   simmering pot. Cook for an additional 5 minutes to blend
   the flavors and serve.

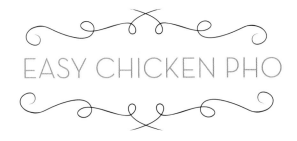

EASY CHICKEN PHO

Ever had Vietnamese food? If not, you should! Then give our Easy Chicken Pho a try and see just how simple it is to have pho at home. To make this recipe even easier, try to find pho soup broth at your local store and have half the work done for you!

PREP TIME: **15 minutes**
COOK TIME: **1 hour**
SERVES: **4 people**

INGREDIENTS:

Broth

1 tablespoon sesame oil

1 white onion, diced

2 cloves garlic, minced

1-inch cube ginger, minced

1 quart chicken broth

¼ cup fish sauce

Hot sauce (optional, sriracha works best)

1 tablespoon salt

1 tablespoon garlic powder

½ tablespoon black pepper

1 teaspoon ground cinnamon

1 teaspoon ground coriander

1 teaspoon ground star anise

Vegetables, Chicken and Herbs

1 large daikon radish

Juice of 1 lime

12 ounces boneless, skinless chicken thighs

INSTRUCTIONS:

1. To make the broth, heat the sesame oil in a soup pot over medium heat, add the onion and cook until it's translucent, about 5 minutes.

2. Add the garlic and ginger and cook until they're fragrant, about 3 minutes.

3. Add the chicken broth, fish sauce and hot sauce to taste and stir to combine.

4. Add the salt, garlic powder, pepper, cinnamon, coriander and star anise, stir well and try a taste. Adjust the seasonings as desired and bring to a gentle boil.

5. To make the vegetables, chicken and herbs, trim the head and end off the daikon radish and peel the outer layer. Spiralize it into thin noodles and drop the noodles into the boiling soup. Add the lime juice and let everything cook for about 15 minutes.

6. Meanwhile, place the chicken thighs on a clean work surface and pound them with a meat tenderizer or rolling pin until they are about ½ inch thick.

7. Heat the olive oil in a skillet over medium-high heat, add the chicken thighs and fry for 5 to 7 minutes on each side or until golden on the outside and firm to the touch.

8. Remove the chicken thighs from the pan and shred them with two forks.

1 tablespoon olive oil

1 fresh jalapeño, sliced
  (optional)

2 scallions, chopped

1 bunch fresh mint leaves,
  chopped

1 bunch fresh parsley leaves,
  chopped

Bean sprouts, for serving

9. Add the shredded chicken to the broth and allow it to heat up for about 10 minutes to absorb some of the broth flavors.

10. To serve, divide the broth among 4 bowls and garnish with the jalapeño, scallion, fresh mint, parsley and bean sprouts.

PORK AND KALE STEW

Pork and Kale Stew is savory, warm meal for the coldest winter nights, made with robust pork, kale and hearty vegetables. It's best enjoyed with a good dollop of sour cream to finish it off!

PREP TIME: 15 minutes
COOK TIME: 4 hours
SERVES: 6–8 people

INGREDIENTS:

2 tablespoons olive oil

1 white onion, chopped

2 large carrots, sliced

3 stalks celery, chopped

20 ounces pork shoulder, cubed

1 quart chicken broth

1 quart water

2 teaspoons salt

2 teaspoons whole peppercorns

1 teaspoon dried oregano

1 teaspoon dried basil

5 bay leaves

1 pound fresh kale, stemmed, leaves chopped

1 butternut squash

Sour cream, for serving

INSTRUCTIONS:

1. Heat the olive oil in a large soup pot over medium heat, add the onion and cook until it is translucent, about 5 minutes.

2. Add the carrots and celery and let them cook for about 10 minutes, until they are a bit softened.

3. Transfer the veggies to a bowl, add the pork to the pot and sear the cubes for about a minute on all sides. This may take 2 or 3 batches, depending on the size of your soup pot.

4. Once complete, deglaze the pan by adding a bit of chicken broth and scraping the leftover pieces with a wooden spoon. Add all the vegetables back in as well as the rest of the chicken broth and water.

5. Season the stew with the salt, peppercorns, oregano, basil and bay leaves and bring it to a boil.

6. Lower the heat to a simmer and add the kale.

7. Let the soup simmer for about 3 hours, adding more water occasionally if necessary.

8. In the last 30 minutes of cooking, cut off the bulbous half of the butternut squash. Cut the end of the straighter half off and peel its hard skin multiple times until you reach the bright orange inside. Spiralize the squash into thick noodles and add them to the stew.

9. Remove the bay leaves before serving.

10. Serve with an optional dollop of sour cream.

CUCUMBER MINT SALAD

Our Cucumber Mint Salad is a refreshing pairing to any dinner recipe.
Cucumber and mint cool you down while yogurt adds the perfect amount of tang.

PREP TIME: **10 minutes**
COOK TIME: **0 minutes**
SERVES: **4 people**

INGREDIENTS:

2 large cucumbers

¼ cup chopped red onion

½ cup whole milk yogurt

5 or 6 large fresh mint leaves,
    plus 1 for garnish

½ teaspoon salt

½ teaspoon dried dill

2 tablespoons olive oil

½ tablespoon white vinegar

INSTRUCTIONS:

1. Spiralize the cucumbers into ribbons and add them to a mixing bowl.

2. Add the chopped red onion and yogurt and toss to combine.

3. Roughly chop the mint leaves and add them to the mixing bowl along with the salt, dill, olive oil and vinegar. Toss well to combine and garnish with a fresh mint leaf.

HONEY BALSAMIC SKIRT STEAK SALAD

If you like balsamic vinegar and haven't tried it yet with steak, it's a must! The secret to this Honey Balsamic Skirt Steak Salad is the balsamic vinegar and honey marinade.

PREP TIME: **15** minutes
COOK TIME: **15** minutes
SERVES: **4** people

INGREDIENTS:

Marinade and Steak

¼ cup olive oil

2 tablespoons balsamic vinegar

2 tablespoons honey

1 teaspoon salt

½ teaspoon black pepper

24 ounces skirt steak

Salad

2 pears

1 teaspoon lemon juice

3 cups fresh arugula

2 ounces roasted cashews (whole or chopped)

2 tablespoons olive oil

Salt

2 ounces blue cheese, crumbled

INSTRUCTIONS:

1. To make the marinade and steak, whisk together the oil, vinegar, honey, salt and pepper in a wide, shallow dish. Add the steak, turn to coat it with the marinade and let marinate in the refrigerator for at least 2 hours or preferably overnight.

2. Heat a skillet over medium-high heat and sear the steak for about 7 minutes on each side or until slightly pink when sliced with a knife. Transfer to a plate, cover with foil and let rest for about 5 minutes to reabsorb all its juices.

3. To make the salad, remove the stems from the pears and spiralize them into thin noodles. Transfer the noodles to a serving bowl. Add the lemon juice to the bowl to prevent browning and toss the noodles to coat them.

4. Add the arugula and roasted cashews.

5. Dress the salad with the olive oil and salt and toss to combine.

6. Slice the skirt steak into thin strips.

7. Divide the salad among 4 plates and add the skirt steak strips equally to each.

8. Add the crumbled blue cheese on top and serve.

GREEK LEMON CHICKEN AND BEET SALAD

Lemon, feta, capers and chicken make Greek Lemon Chicken and Beet Salad
a classic recipe with flavors originating from the Mediterranean. We incorporated
beets and cucumbers for a lovely crunch and volume.

PREP TIME: **10 minutes**
COOK TIME: **12 minutes**
SERVES: **4 people**

INGREDIENTS:

12 ounces boneless, skinless chicken breasts

3 tablespoons olive oil

Salt and pepper

2 medium beets

2 large cucumbers

Juice of 1 lemon

4 ounces feta cheese

1 tablespoon capers, for garnish

INSTRUCTIONS:

1. Place the chicken breasts on a clean work surface and pound them with a meat tenderizer or rolling pin until they're about ½ inch thick.

2. Heat 1 tablespoon of the olive oil in a large pan over medium-high heat and sauté the chicken breasts for 5 to 7 minutes on each side or until golden on the outside and the juices run clear when cut.

3. Season with salt and pepper to taste on each side.

4. Trim any leaves and stems off the beets and peel them. Use gloves to prevent your fingers from staining. Spiralize the beets into thin noodles.

5. Cut the ends off the cucumbers and spiralize them into thick noodles.

6. Add all the noodles to a mixing bowl and toss with the remaining 2 tablespoons of olive oil.

7. Add the freshly squeezed lemon juice and feta cheese to the mixing bowl.

8. Once the chicken breasts are ready, remove them from the pan, shred them with two forks and add them to the mix.

9. Toss the salad and divide it among 4 plates. Garnish with the capers and serve.

RAINBOW SALAD

Nutritionists say to eat colorful veggies every day, and that's easy to do with our Rainbow Salad! Bursts of flavor and fun textures mean this salad will satisfy your taste buds while supplying your nutrients in as well.

PREP TIME: 15 minutes
COOK TIME: 0 minutes
SERVES: 4–6 people

INGREDIENTS:

2 medium zucchini

2 yellow squash

2 medium carrots

1 head of red cabbage

4 Campari tomatoes, diced

¾ cup ranch dressing

Chopped fresh parsley,
    for garnish

INSTRUCTIONS:

1. Trim the ends off the zucchini, yellow squash and carrots. Peel the carrots and spiralize all three vegetables into thin noodles. Add the noodles to a large bowl.

2. Using the ribbon attachment on your spiralizer, shred the red cabbage and add it to the bowl along with the diced tomatoes.

3. Dress the Rainbow Salad with the ranch dressing and toss to combine everything well.

4. Garnish the salad with fresh parsley and serve.

SEARED TUNA AVOCADO SALAD

Tuna is best raw! Our Seared Tuna Avocado Salad adds Asian-inspired flavors to the dish and really brings out the savory flavors raw tuna has to offer.

PREP TIME: **15 minutes**
COOK TIME: **2 minutes**
SERVES: **4 people**

INGREDIENTS:

4 (6-ounce) ahi tuna steaks

Salt and pepper

1 tablespoon toasted sesame oil or olive oil

2 medium carrots

2 medium cucumbers

½ cup shelled edamame

2 avocados, peeled, pitted and thinly sliced

¼ cup soy sauce

3 tablespoons lime juice

Roasted seaweed, ripped

Black and white sesame seeds

INSTRUCTIONS:

1. Dry the ahi tuna steaks with a paper towel and season them with salt and pepper.

2. Place a large cast-iron skillet or large deep pan over high heat. Once it's almost smoking, add the toasted sesame oil and the tuna steaks. Let them sear for about a minute or two on each side. Remove the tuna from the pan and let them rest on a plate while you prepare the rest of the salad.

3. Trim the ends off the carrots, peel them and spiralize them into thin noodles.

4. Trim the ends off the cucumbers and spiralize them into thin noodles.

5. Divide the noodles among 4 plates and top with an even amount of shelled edamame and ½ of an avocado.

6. Cut the tuna steaks into thin slices and place them on top of each salad.

7. Drizzle each salad with equal amounts of the soy sauce and lime juice.

8. Add the roasted seaweed shreds and season with salt and pepper to taste.

9. Garnish with the black and white sesame seeds and serve.

SHREDDED CHICKEN AND PEAR SALAD

Shredded Chicken and Pear Salad is one of our go-to salads in the spring and summer. It's tangy, sour and sweet and quite filling, so it is great as a lunch or even dinner.

PREP TIME: **10** minutes
COOK TIME: **12** minutes
SERVES: **4** people

INGREDIENTS:

12 ounces boneless, skinless chicken breasts

¼ cup olive oil

2 pears

2 tablespoons fresh lemon juice

4 ounces spinach

⅓ cup dried cranberries

Salt and pepper

4 ounces goat cheese

INSTRUCTIONS:

1. Place the chicken breasts on a clean work surface and pound them with a meat tenderizer or rolling pin until they're about ½ inch thick.

2. Heat 1 tablespoon of the olive oil in a large pan over medium-high heat and sauté the chicken breasts for 5 to 7 minutes on each side or until golden on the outside and the juices run clear when cut.

3. Remove the chicken from the pan and shred the meat with two forks. Add the shredded chicken to a large mixing bowl.

4. Remove the stems from the pears and spiralize them into thin noodles. Add the pear noodles to the mixing bowl.

5. Add the lemon juice, spinach, dried cranberries, salt and pepper to taste, 2 ounces of the goat cheese, crumbled, and the remaining 3 tablespoons of olive oil to the mixing bowl and toss well.

6. Divide the salad among 4 plates, crumble the remaining 2 ounces of goat cheese on top and serve.

WALDORF SALAD

This Waldorf Salad is closely related to a traditional chicken salad but includes crisp, juicy apple noodles. The salad is sweet and tangy and is a great lunch to take to work or school!

PREP TIME: 10 minutes
COOK TIME: 0 minutes
SERVES: 4 people

INGREDIENTS:

1 heart of romaine lettuce

1 apple

Juice of 1 lemon

1 cup red grapes, sliced in half

½ cup whole walnuts

2 stalks celery

12 ounces cooked boneless, skinless chicken breasts, shredded

½ cup mayonnaise

Salt and pepper

INSTRUCTIONS:

1. Rinse the romaine lettuce heart and slice widthwise into 1-inch strips.

2. Remove the stem from the apple and spiralize it into thin noodles. Place the apple noodles in a bowl and squeeze a bit of lemon juice over them to prevent browning.

3. Combine the lettuce and apple noodles in a large bowl and add the grapes and walnuts.

4. Chop the celery and add it to the bowl along with the shredded chicken breast.

5. Dress the salad with the remaining lemon juice and the mayonnaise.

6. Season with salt and pepper to taste and toss very well to combine.

BEET AND ORANGE SALAD

A quick and simple salad that combines earthy and sweet flavors perfectly, Beet and Orange Salad will brighten up your mood on a cold winter day!

PREP TIME: 20 minutes
COOK TIME: 0 minutes
SERVES: 4 people

INGREDIENTS:

3 beets

2 navel oranges

½ cup slivered almonds

Salt

Honey Mustard Vinaigrette

¼ cup mustard

¼ cup honey

½ cup olive oil

2 tablespoons white vinegar

Salt and pepper

INSTRUCTIONS:

1. Trim any leaves and stems off the beets and peel them. Use gloves to prevent your fingers from staining. Spiralize the beets into thin noodles and place them in a deep mixing bowl.

2. Peel the navel oranges and add the slices to the mixing bowl along with the slivered almonds. Season with salt to taste and stir to combine.

3. Divide the salad among 4 plates.

4. To make the vinaigrette, whisk together the vinaigrette ingredients in a small bowl and drizzle it over each portion of salad. Serve immediately

BUFFALO CHICKEN SLAW

Buffalo Chicken Slaw became our go-to lazy lunch after the first time we tried it. It provides meat and veggies all in one bowl with very little prep necessary, making it a winner in our eyes.

PREP TIME: 10 minutes
COOK TIME: 15 minutes
SERVES: 4 people

INGREDIENTS:

2 boneless, skinless chicken thighs

1 tablespoon olive oil

1 head of white cabbage

1 large carrot

2 stalks celery, chopped

½ cup mayonnaise

Salt and pepper

¼ cup Buffalo sauce

¼ cup blue cheese dressing

INSTRUCTIONS:

1. Place the chicken thighs on a clean work surface and pound them with a meat tenderizer or rolling pin until they're about ½ inch thick.

2. Heat the olive oil in a large pan over medium-high heat and sauté the chicken thighs for 5 to 7 minutes on each side or until golden and firm to the touch.

3. In the meantime, using the ribbon attachment on your spiralizer, shred the cabbage. Place it in a deep mixing bowl.

4. Trim the ends off the carrot, peel it and spiralize it into thick noodles. Cut the noodles with kitchen shears to make short segments. Add them to the shredded cabbage.

5. Add the chopped celery and mayonnaise. Season with salt and pepper to taste.

6. Remove the chicken thighs from the pan and shred them with two forks. Add them to the slaw.

7. Pour in the Buffalo sauce and blue cheese dressing. Toss until everything is well combined.

8. Serve the Buffalo Chicken Slaw chilled for best flavor.

STRAWBERRY PECAN SALAD

A little sweetness can go a long way with our Strawberry Pecan Salad! Dive into the bursts of flavors from sweet strawberries, tangy goat cheese and salty pecans.

PREP TIME: 5 minutes
COOK TIME: 0 minutes
SERVES: 4 people

INGREDIENTS:

2 medium cucumbers

2 cups fresh arugula

8 ounces strawberries, sliced

2 ounces goat cheese

2 ounces roasted and salted pecans

1 tablespoon chia seeds

1 to 2 tablespoons mild-flavored oil (such as avocado)

1 to 2 tablespoons balsamic vinegar

INSTRUCTIONS:

1. Trim the ends off the cucumbers and spiralize them into ribbons. Place the ribbons in a mixing bowl along with the arugula. You may want to cut the cucumber ribbons into smaller strips.

2. Add the sliced strawberries and crumble the goat cheese over the top.

3. Add the pecans and chia seeds, drizzle the salad with the oil and vinegar, toss the ingredients gently to combine and serve.

CALIFORNIA CHICKEN SALAD

Avocados and walnuts from California are delicious! Their healthy fats contribute to the fullness factor of this California Chicken Salad. Along with raw broccoli stems, cherry tomatoes and romaine hearts, this salad provides a ton of nutrients in one bowl!

PREP TIME: **15** minutes
COOK TIME: **12** minutes
SERVES: **4** people

INGREDIENTS:

10 ounces boneless, skinless chicken breasts

3 tablespoons olive oil

1 heart of romaine lettuce

2 broccoli stems

1 cup cherry tomatoes

8 slices bacon, cooked and crumbled

1 avocado, peeled, pitted and cubed

½ cup chopped walnuts

2 tablespoons white vinegar

Juice of 1 lemon

INSTRUCTIONS:

1. Place the chicken breasts on a clean work surface and pound them with a meat tenderizer or rolling pin until they're about ½ inch thick.

2. Heat 1 tablespoon of the olive oil in a large pan over medium-high heat and sauté the chicken breasts for 5 to 7 minutes on each side or until golden on the outside and the juices run clear when cut.

3. In the meantime, rinse the romaine lettuce heart and slice widthwise into 1-inch-thick slices. Add the slices to a mixing bowl.

4. Trim off any dry ends of the broccoli stems and peel them lightly. Spiralize them into ribbons and add them to the mixing bowl.

5. Remove the chicken breasts from the pan and shred them with two forks.

6. Add the cherry tomatoes, shredded chicken breasts and crumbled bacon to the mixing bowl.

7. Add the avocado chunks to the mixing bowl along with the walnuts.

8. Dress the California Chicken Salad with the remaining 2 tablespoons of olive oil, vinegar and lemon juice. Toss the ingredients gently to coat, and serve.

WARM POMEGRANATE SQUASH SALAD

Squash isn't just for fall, especially when it goes so perfectly in this Warm Pomegranate Squash Salad! Roasting butternut squash brings out extra flavor and a warm pear is an absolute treat.

PREP TIME: 10 minutes
COOK TIME: 10 minutes
SERVES: 4 people

INGREDIENTS:

1 butternut squash

2 pears

5 tablespoons olive oil

2 cups fresh arugula

½ cup pomegranate seeds

⅓ cup shelled pumpkin seeds

1 tablespoon balsamic
    vinegar

Salt

INSTRUCTIONS:

1. Preheat the oven to 350°F. Line a 13 x 9-inch baking sheet with aluminum foil.

2. Cut the bulbous end off the butternut squash and then peel the outer hard skin multiple times until you get to the bright orange inside. Spiralize the squash into thin noodles.

3. Remove the stems from the pears and spiralize them into thin noodles.

4. Combine the butternut squash noodles and pear noodles in a bowl, drizzle with 1 tablespoon of the olive oil and toss to coat.

5. Spread the noodles in an even layer on the prepared baking sheet and bake for 10 minutes. The outer edges of the noodles should be slightly browned.

6. Transfer the noodles to a mixing bowl along with the arugula, pomegranate seeds and pumpkin seeds. Toss everything to combine well.

7. Dress the salad with the remaining 4 tablespoons of olive oil, balsamic vinegar and salt to taste.

PULLED PORK AND APPLE SALAD

Our Pulled Pork and Apple Salad combines creamy, meaty and crunchy textures. The lemony vinaigrette adds the perfect amount of kick to the flavorful pork and juicy apples.

PREP TIME: 10 minutes
COOK TIME: 0 minutes
SERVES: 4 people

INGREDIENTS:

Salad

4 cups fresh arugula

1 Fuji apple

2 avocados, cored, peeled and sliced

12 ounces cooked pulled pork

2 ounces pecans, crushed or whole

Lemon Vinaigrette

Juice of ½ lemon

2 tablespoons balsamic vinegar

1 teaspoon salt

½ teaspoon pepper

¼ cup olive oil

INSTRUCTIONS:

1. To make the salad, arrange the arugula in a bed on each of 4 plates.

2. Remove the stem from the apple and spiralize it into ribbons. Arrange the ribbons nicely on the beds of arugula.

3. Lay out half an avocado in slices on each plate.

4. Add the pulled pork to each serving and sprinkle the pecans on top.

5. To make the vinaigrette, combine the lemon juice, vinegar, salt and pepper in a small bowl and whisk to blend. While whisking, drizzle in the olive oil slowly to form an emulsion.

6. Drizzle the Pulled Pork and Apple Salad with the Lemon Vinaigrette and serve.

TILAPIA DAIKON NOODLE SALAD

Daikon noodles are awesome! They bring so much texture and crunch to the table (pun intended) and really give this Tilapia Daikon Noodle Salad a great balance. Have it for lunch or dinner: you won't be disappointed!

PREP TIME: **10 minutes**
COOK TIME: **15 minutes**
SERVES: **4 people**

INGREDIENTS:

1 daikon radish

1 large carrot

2 tablespoons olive oil

1 pound fresh tilapia

2 Campari tomatoes, diced

Juice of 1 lemon

Salt and pepper

Chopped fresh parsley, for garnish

INSTRUCTIONS:

1. Trim the ends off the daikon radish and carrot and peel their top layers. Spiralize them both into thick noodles.

2. Heat the olive oil in a large skillet over medium heat, add the tilapia and fry on each side for 5 to 7 minutes or until it can be easily flaked with a fork and is opaque throughout.

3. During the last 5 minutes, add the daikon and carrot noodles to the pan.

4. Toss everything gently and you should see the tilapia breaking down into bite-size pieces.

5. Add the diced tomatoes to a large mixing bowl along with the lemon juice.

6. Add the tilapia, daikon and carrots to the mixing bowl and season everything with salt and pepper.

7. Mix everything together well, garnish the salad with the chopped fresh parsley and serve.

LEMON THYME SALMON AND DILL CUCUMBER SALAD

Fresh herbs are the way to go! They add immense flavor without any added calories. We chose fresh thyme to complement the salmon and sweeten up the acidity the lemon juice provides in this Lemon Thyme Salmon and Dill Cucumber Salad.

PREP TIME: 10 minutes
COOK TIME: 12 minutes
SERVES: 4 people

INGREDIENTS:

1 tablespoon olive oil

4 (8-ounce) salmon fillets

Salt and pepper

4 sprigs fresh thyme

Juice of 1 lemon

2 large cucumbers

¼ cup sour cream

1 teaspoon dried dill

2 tablespoons capers, for garnish

INSTRUCTIONS:

1. Heat the oil in a large skillet on high heat until it gets very hot.

2. Pat the salmon fillets dry and season them with salt and pepper.

3. Place the fillets skin side down in the skillet and cook them for about 5 minutes.

4. Flip each fillet and add the fresh thyme sprigs and lemon juice. Cook them for 5 more minutes or until they can be flaked easily with a fork.

5. Meanwhile, trim the ends off the cucumbers and peel them.

6. Spiralize the cucumbers into ribbons and combine them in a bowl with the sour cream, dill and salt and pepper to taste. Toss the ribbons to coat them with the dressing and divide them among 4 plates.

7. Place a fillet atop each plate of salad and garnish with the capers.

KALE WALNUT PESTO SALAD
WITH SPIRALIZED APPLE

Kale is a super nutritious green packed with vitamins B$_6$, B$_2$, B$_1$ and E as well as fiber, calcium, omega-3 fatty acids, iron, magnesium and much more! Our Kale Walnut Pesto Salad with Spiralized Apple is a healthy and delicious dish you can make any time.

PREP TIME: **10 minutes**
COOK TIME: **0 minutes**
SERVES: **4 people**

INGREDIENTS:

4 cups chopped fresh kale, stemmed

¼ cup olive oil

Salt and pepper

2 Granny Smith apples

1 tablespoon lemon juice

2 tablespoons pesto

½ cup toasted walnuts

INSTRUCTIONS:

1. Toss the kale in a deep mixing bowl with the olive oil and a big pinch of salt. Massage the leaves with your hands for about 3 minutes to soften the kale and reduce the bitterness.

2. Remove the stems from the apples and spiralize them into ribbons. In a small bowl, combine the apple ribbons with the lemon juice to prevent browning.

3. Add the apple ribbons, pesto, walnuts and salt and pepper to taste to the softened kale and toss to combine. Serve immediately.

ZESTY SHRIMP AVOCADO SALAD

This Zesty Shrimp Avocado Salad is a fresh summer dish with a little kick! We love the combination of shrimp, avocado and lime. It's juicy, sweet and spicy all at the same time.

PREP TIME: 15 minutes
COOK TIME: 8 minutes
SERVES: 4 people

INGREDIENTS:

Shrimp

1 tablespoon olive oil

12 ounces large shrimp

½ teaspoon paprika

Pinch of cayenne (optional)

Juice of ½ lime

Salt and pepper

Salad

1 medium cucumber

1 medium carrot

¼ cup mayonnaise

1 tablespoon soy sauce

2 teaspoons sriracha (optional)

1 avocado, peeled, pitted and diced

Salt and pepper

INSTRUCTIONS:

1. To make the shrimp, heat the olive oil in a large pan over high heat. Add the shrimp and cook for 3 to 4 minutes on each side, until they are completely pink and opaque.

2. Season the shrimp with the paprika, cayenne, lime juice and salt and pepper to taste. Stir to coat the shrimp fully and then remove the pan from the heat.

3. To make the salad, trim the ends off the cucumber and carrot and peel them.

4. Spiralize both vegetables into thin noodles, transfer to a mixing bowl and add the mayonnaise, soy sauce, sriracha and diced avocado. Season with salt and pepper to taste and toss gently to combine.

5. Add the cooked shrimp and toss gently again.

6. Divide the salad among 4 plates and serve.

PESTO CHICKEN BUTTERNUT RIBBON SALAD

Two strong flavors combine to create a new type of sauce we're excited to share. Bold basil pesto and tangy mayonnaise turn this Pesto Chicken Butternut Ribbon Salad into an easy lunch or dinner delicacy.

PREP TIME: 10 minutes
COOK TIME: 25 minutes
SERVES: 4–6 people

INGREDIENTS:

Pesto

1 cup fresh basil leaves

2 tablespoons pine nuts

2 tablespoons grated Parmesan cheese

1 clove garlic

Salt and pepper

¼ cup olive oil

Noodles and Chicken

2 butternut squash

1 pound boneless, skinless chicken thighs

2 tablespoons olive oil

3 large Roma tomatoes, diced

¼ cup mayonnaise

1 teaspoon dried basil, for garnish

INSTRUCTIONS:

1. Preheat the oven to 450°F. Line a 13 x 9-inch baking sheet with foil and grease the foil.

2. To make the pesto, combine the basil, pine nuts, Parmesan, garlic and salt and pepper to taste in a food processor and blend them until they are smooth.

3. While blending, pour the olive oil in a slow stream to create an emulsion, or just pour in about 1 tablespoon of olive oil at a time.

4. To make the noodles, cut off the ends of the butternut squash. Peel the straighter half until you reach the bright orange inside. Spiralize the squash into ribbons.

5. Spread ribbons onto baking sheet and bake for 15 minutes or until the edges are slightly browned.

6. Meanwhile, place the chicken thighs on a clean work surface and pound them with a meat tenderizer or rolling pin until they're about ½ inch thick.

7. Heat the olive oil in a large pan over medium-high heat and sauté the chicken thighs for 5 to 7 minutes on each side or until they are golden and firm to the touch.

8. Remove the chicken from the pan, shred the meat and add it to a deep mixing bowl along with the squash ribbons.

9. Add the diced tomatoes, pesto and mayonnaise to the bowl. Toss everything very well to combine.

10. Garnish with the dried basil and serve.

SUMMER SALAD

There's something about the combination of fresh summer fruit and a tangy lemon vinaigrette. Make a batch of this Summer Salad for lunch or a barbecue. You can enjoy this salad year-round, but the flavor is best when the fruit is in season.

PREP TIME: 15 minutes
COOK TIME: 0 minutes
SERVES: 4 people

INGREDIENTS:

4 cups fresh arugula

2 cups sliced strawberries

1 cup blueberries

1 apple

½ red onion

Lemon Vinaigrette

Juice of ½ lemon

2 tablespoons balsamic vinegar

1 teaspoon salt

½ teaspoon pepper

¼ cup olive oil

INSTRUCTIONS:

1. Add the arugula, sliced strawberries and blueberries to a deep mixing bowl.

2. Remove the stem from the apple and spiralize it into ribbons. Add it to the bowl.

3. Shred the red onion using the ribbon attachment on your spiralizer and add it to the bowl.

4. To make the Lemon Vinaigrette, combine the lemon juice, vinegar, salt and pepper in a small bowl and whisk it all together.

5. While whisking, drizzle in the olive oil slowly to form an emulsion.

6. Drizzle the salad with the vinaigrette and serve.

STEAK AND ALMOND PESTO ZOODLES

Pesto is a great way of adding flair to any dish and is the perfect complement to steak. The basil pesto in this Steak and Almond Pesto Zoodles dish uses almonds instead of pine nuts for a slightly different flavor. Almonds are also much more accessible than pine nuts, so if you've only got almonds on hand, you're in luck!

PREP TIME: 20 minutes
COOK TIME: 15 minutes
SERVES: 4 people

INGREDIENTS:

Steak and Zoodles

Salt and pepper

1 pound flank steak

2 large zucchini

1 tablespoon olive oil

Pesto

1 cup fresh basil, plus more for garnish

¼ cup sliced almonds, plus more for garnish

2 tablespoons Parmesan cheese, plus more for garnish

1 clove garlic

¼ cup olive oil

INSTRUCTIONS:

1. To make the steak and zoodles, liberally season the flank steak with salt and let it sit for at least an hour. This will help tenderize the meat for a softer result.

2. Preheat the broiler and place the steak on a baking sheet about 6 inches from the heat. Depending on the thickness of the steak, it should take about 5 minutes on each side. Check the internal temperature of the steak with an instant-read thermometer; for medium-rare, the temperature should be 125°F. Remove the steak from the oven and allow it to rest on a plate at room temperature for about 5 minutes.

3. Trim the ends off the zucchini and spiralize them into thick noodles. Heat the olive oil in a skillet over medium-low heat, add the zoodles and cook them for about 2 minutes, tossing continuously. Season the zoodles with salt and pepper to taste. Transfer the zoodles to a large bowl.

4. To make the pesto, combine the basil, almonds, Parmesan and garlic in a food processor and blend until they are smooth.

5. While blending, slowly pour in the olive oil to create an emulsion. If you can't pour while blending, just pour in about 1 tablespoon of oil at a time and blend after each addition. Add about 2 tablespoons of the pesto to the zucchini noodles and toss to mix them together.

6. After the steak has had a chance to rest, slice it into thin strips and serve it alongside the pesto zoodles. Garnish the Steak and Almond Pesto Zoodles with the rest of the pesto, Parmesan cheese, almonds and fresh basil.

ASIAN SALMON SESAME SALAD

There's nothing better than a bright and flavorful Asian Salmon Sesame Salad for lunch! We always enjoy this delicious mix of creamy avocado, salty soy sauce and sweet and spicy ginger.

PREP TIME: **15 minutes**
COOK TIME: **10 minutes**
SERVES: **4 people**

INGREDIENTS:

2 tablespoons olive oil

12 ounces salmon fillets

2 medium cucumbers

2 medium carrots

½-inch cube ginger, grated

1 tablespoon soy sauce

2 avocados, peeled, pitted and sliced

Black and white sesame seeds, for garnish

INSTRUCTIONS:

1. Heat the olive oil in a large skillet over medium heat, add the salmon and fry for 4 to 6 minutes on each side, depending on thickness of the fillets. They should flake easily with a fork.

2. Trim the ends off the cucumbers and spiralize them into thin noodles.

3. Trim the ends off the carrots, peel them and spiralize them into thin noodles.

4. Add the grated ginger, carrot noodles and cucumber noodles to a mixing bowl and drizzle them with the soy sauce. Toss to coat everything evenly and divide the salad among 4 plates.

5. Shred the cooked salmon with a fork and sprinkle an equal portion onto each salad.

6. Add half a sliced avocado to each plate and garnish with the black and white sesame seeds.

MEXICAN JICAMA SALAD

Jicama is a native Mexican vine vegetable that tastes great raw or cooked.
When jicama is raw and spiralized, its texture and flavor bear a strong resemblance to
apples, giving Mexican Jicama Salad a great balance of sweet and savory.

PREP TIME: 10 minutes
COOK TIME: 0 minutes
SERVES: 4 people

INGREDIENTS:

1 large jicama

½ red onion, diced

4 Campari tomatoes, diced

2 avocados, pitted, peeled
  and diced

1 jalapeño (optional)

Juice of 1 lime

2 tablespoons olive oil

Salt and pepper

Chopped fresh cilantro, for
  garnish

INSTRUCTIONS:

1. Slice the ends off the jicama and carefully cut off the
   waxy skin with a paring knife. Spiralize the jicama into
   thick noodles.

2. Combine the red onion, tomatoes and avocados with the
   jicama noodles in a large bowl.

3. If using the jalapeño, dice it finely and add it to the bowl.
   Remove the seeds and white membranes for less heat.

4. Add the lime juice, olive oil and salt and pepper to taste
   and toss the salad to combine.

5. Garnish with the cilantro and serve.

APPLE WALNUT GOAT CHEESE SALAD

Apple and goat cheese give our Apple Walnut Goat Cheese Salad a great contrast in flavors for your palate. The salad's speed and ease of preparation means you can enjoy it as a quick lunch or side any time.

PREP TIME: **10** minutes
COOK TIME: **0** minutes
SERVES:**4** people

INGREDIENTS:

1 apple

2 cucumbers

4 cups fresh arugula

2 ounces walnuts, chopped or whole

Juice of ½ lemon

1 tablespoon apple cider vinegar

2 tablespoons olive oil

½ teaspoon salt

4 ounces goat cheese

Lemon slices, for garnish

INSTRUCTIONS:

1. Remove the stem from the apple and spiralize it into thin noodles.

2. Trim the ends off the cucumbers and spiralize them into thin noodles.

3. Add the arugula to a deep mixing bowl along with the apple and cucumber noodles.

4. Add the walnuts, lemon juice, apple cider vinegar and olive oil. Season with the salt and toss the salad well to combine.

5. Divide the salad among 4 plates, crumble the goat cheese on top and garnish with the fresh lemon slices.

SESAME GINGER CARROT SALAD

Simple and light, Sesame Ginger Carrot Salad is great for a quick lunch or midday snack. It packs a lot of flavor and is one of our favorite bites when we don't have much time for lunch.

PREP TIME: 10 minutes
COOK TIME: 0 minutes
SERVES: 4 people

INGREDIENTS:

2 medium carrots

2 medium cucumbers

1 radish

½ cup shelled edamame

Dressing

Juice of 1 lime

1 tablespoon sesame oil
   (or olive oil)

1 tablespoon soy sauce

1 inch cube ginger, grated

Salt and pepper

Garnish

2 sheets roasted seaweed,
   chopped

2 scallions, chopped

INSTRUCTIONS:

1. Trim the ends off the carrots, peel them and spiralize them into thin noodles. Add the noodles to a salad bowl.

2. Trim the ends off the cucumbers and spiralize them into thin noodles. Add the cucumber noodles to the salad bowl.

3. Cut the radish into thin slices and add it to the salad bowl along with the shelled edamame.

4. Combine the dressing ingredients in a small mixing bowl and whisk together until combined.

5. Dress the salad and toss well to coat everything.

6. Divide the salad among 4 plates and garnish with a few pieces of roasted seaweed and a scattering of scallions.

FUJI APPLE, CHICKEN AND KALE SALAD

Kale is our favorite hearty leafy green that we're always trying to add to our salads. You'll love the bold flavors and creamy, salty feta that make Fuji Apple, Chicken and Kale Salad perfect for a cool fall day.

PREP TIME: 10 minutes
COOK TIME: 15 minutes
SERVES: 4 people

INGREDIENTS:

12 ounces boneless, skinless chicken breasts

2 tablespoons olive oil

8 ounces fresh kale

Juice of 1 lemon

Pinch of salt

1 Fuji apple

1 tablespoon apple cider vinegar

2 ounces feta cheese

¼ cup pine nuts

INSTRUCTIONS:

1. Place the chicken breasts on a clean work surface and pound them with a meat tenderizer or rolling pin until they're about ½ inch thick.

2. Heat 1 tablespoon of the olive oil in a large pan over medium-high heat and sauté the chicken breasts for 5 to 7 minutes on each side or until golden on the outside and the juices run clear when cut.

3. In the meantime, place the kale in a deep mixing bowl, drizzle with the lemon juice, remaining 1 tablespoon of olive oil and a big pinch of salt. Massage the leaves with your hands for about 2 minutes to soften the kale and reduce the bitterness.

4. Spiralize the apple into ribbons and add a squirt of lemon juice to prevent browning.

5. Remove the chicken breasts from the pan and shred them with two forks.

6. Add the apple ribbons, shredded chicken and a pinch of salt to the kale salad. Drizzle with the apple cider vinegar and toss to combine the ingredients.

7. Crumble the feta cheese into the bowl, sprinkle on the pine nuts for extra texture and crunch and serve.

GOLDEN BEET AND SUNFLOWER SALAD

The earthy flavor of beets works wonderfully with the sweet and tart flavors of the dressing in Golden Beet and Sunflower Salad. We love to add crunch to salads, so instead of boring croutons, we throw in delicious and healthy nuts and seeds.

PREP TIME: **10 minutes**
COOK TIME: **0 minutes**
SERVES: **4 people**

INGREDIENTS:

2 golden beets (or regular beets)

4 cups fresh arugula

½ red onion, sliced

¼ cup sunflower seeds

Dressing

½ cup full-fat Greek yogurt

2 tablespoons honey

Salt

INSTRUCTIONS:

1. Trim any leaves and stems off the golden beets and peel them. Use gloves to prevent your fingers from staining. Spiralize the beets into thin or thick noodles according to your preference.

2. Add the beet noodles to a mixing bowl along with the arugula.

3. Add the sliced red onion and sunflower seeds.

4. To make the dressing, whisk together the Greek yogurt, honey and salt in a small bowl.

5. Drizzle the dressing over the salad, divide it among 4 plates and serve.

BBQ PORK LOIN SALAD

The bold flavors of pork need something sweet to balance the dish. That's why most barbecue sauces are sweet. We love the combo of apples and cranberry with savory pork and red onion. BBQ Pork Loin Salad is reminiscent of Thanksgiving but a better fit for the summer months!

PREP TIME: 10 minutes
COOK TIME: 0 minutes
SERVES: 4 people

INGREDIENTS:

4 cups spinach

1 apple

½ red onion

1 pound cooked pork loin

⅔ cup barbecue sauce

Salt and pepper

½ cup dried cranberries

INSTRUCTIONS:

1. Make a bed of spinach on each of 4 plates.

2. Spiralize the apple into ribbons and arrange the ribbons nicely on the beds of spinach.

3. Spiralize the red onion half using the ribbon attachment on your spiralizer and add the ribbons to the salad.

4. Shred the pork loin using two forks, add it to a bowl, pour in the barbecue sauce and toss to combine. Let the pork rest for a few minutes to soak up the flavors.

5. Top the salads with the pork, season with salt and pepper to taste and toss everything to combine.

6. Sprinkle the salads with the dried cranberries and serve.

BEET AND GOAT CHEESE ARUGULA SALAD

Roasted beets make a crispy treat in our Beet and Goat Cheese Arugula Salad. The vinaigrette gives the salad a sweet glaze and complements all the flavors.

PREP TIME: 20 minutes
COOK TIME: 10 minutes
SERVES: 4 people

INGREDIENTS:

Vinaigrette

¼ cup balsamic vinegar

1 tablespoon honey

¼ cup olive oil

Salt and pepper

Salad

4 medium beets

8 ounces fresh arugula

¼ cup toasted walnuts

¼ cup cranberries

2 ounces goat cheese

INSTRUCTIONS:

1. Preheat the oven to 450°F. Line a 13 x 9-inch baking sheet with foil and grease the foil.

2. To make the vinaigrette, whisk the balsamic vinegar and honey together in a small bowl. Whisk in the olive oil gradually until the ingredients are well combined. Add salt and pepper to taste and stir to combine.

3. To make the salad, trim any leaves and stems off the beets and peel them. Use gloves to prevent your fingers from staining. Spiralize the beets into thick noodles.

4. In a large mixing bowl, toss the beet noodles with half of the vinaigrette.

5. Spread the coated beet noodles on the prepared baking sheet and roast them for about 10 minutes, or until they slightly caramelize.

6. In the same mixing bowl, toss the arugula, walnuts and cranberries with the remaining half of the vinaigrette.

7. Divide the beet noodles evenly among 4 plates and place the tossed salad on top. Crumble the goat cheese on top and serve.

MAIN DISHES

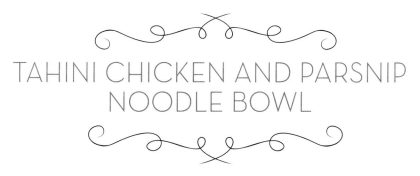

TAHINI CHICKEN AND PARSNIP NOODLE BOWL

Tahini is simply ground sesame seeds. The result is something like a nut butter with a hint of sesame. It's a great nut-free alternative for people with allergies and works well in Tahini Chicken and Parsnip Noodle Bowl.

PREP TIME: **15 minutes**
COOK TIME: **20 minutes**
SERVES: **4–6 people**

INGREDIENTS:

24 ounces boneless, skinless chicken breasts

2 tablespoons olive oil

2 large parsnips

Tahini Dressing

¼ cup tahini

2 teaspoons honey

Juice of ½ lemon

2 cloves garlic

2 tablespoons olive oil

2 tablespoons water

Salt and pepper

Sesame seeds, for garnish

INSTRUCTIONS:

1. On a clean surface, pound the chicken breasts with a meat tenderizer or rolling pin until they're about ½ inch thick.

2. Heat 1½ tablespoons of the olive oil in a large pan over medium-high heat. Sauté the chicken breasts for 5 to 7 minutes on each side or until golden on the outside and the juices run clear when cut. Transfer the chicken to a bowl and shred with two forks.

3. Meanwhile, trim the ends off the parsnips and spiralize them into thick noodles.

4. Heat ½ tablespoon of oil in a skillet over medium heat, add the parsnip noodles and cook for 4 to 5 minutes.

5. To make the Tahini Dressing, add the tahini, honey, lemon juice, garlic, oil, water and salt and pepper to taste to a food processor and blend the ingredients until smooth.

6. Place the shredded chicken, parsnip noodles and tahini dressing in a bowl and toss to combine.

7. Garnish with the sesame seeds and serve.

CHICKEN SQUASH ALFREDO

You don't have to give up Alfredo sauce when you go low carb—it's already low carb, especially if you make it yourself and make sure no flour or thickeners are added. Enjoy our Chicken Squash Alfredo over yellow squash noodles in this ultra-low-carb recipe.

PREP TIME: 15 minutes
COOK TIME: 20 minutes
SERVES: 4 people

INGREDIENTS:

Chicken and Noodles

1 pound boneless, skinless chicken breasts

1 tablespoon olive oil

2 large yellow squash

8 fresh basil leaves, for garnish

Alfredo Sauce

4 tablespoons unsalted butter

4 cloves garlic, crushed

½ cup heavy cream

6 tablespoons grated Parmesan cheese, plus more for garnish

Salt and pepper

INSTRUCTIONS:

1. To make the chicken and noodles, place the chicken breasts on a clean work surface and pound them with a meat tenderizer or rolling pin until they're about ½ inch thick.

2. Heat the olive oil in a large pan over medium heat and sauté the chicken breasts for 5 to 7 minutes on each side or until golden on the outside and the juices run clear when cut. Remove the chicken from the pan and transfer it to a plate while you prepare the sauce and noodles.

3. To make the sauce, in the same pan, melt the butter over low heat and then add the crushed garlic and heavy cream. Let this simmer for 3 minutes.

4. Add the Parmesan cheese 1 tablespoon at a time, waiting until each is incorporated, while mixing continuously. Season with salt and pepper and let the sauce simmer for an additional 5 minutes. The sauce should be pretty thick at this point.

5. Trim the ends off the yellow squash and spiralize it into thick noodles. Add the squash noodles to the pan and cook in the sauce for about 5 minutes.

6. Shred the chicken breast with two forks and add it to the pan. Toss everything to coat it in the sauce.

7. Garnish the Chicken Squash Alfredo with more Parmesan cheese and chopped fresh basil.

GINGER CHICKEN STIR-FRY

Asian flair shines through in Ginger Chicken Stir-Fry! Toasted sesame oil gives the dish authentic flavor while ginger adds a delicate sweetness to the robust ingredients.

PREP TIME: 5 minutes
COOK TIME: 15 minutes
SERVES: 4 people

INGREDIENTS:

1 pound boneless, skinless chicken breasts

2 tablespoons olive oil, divided

½-inch cube ginger, grated

1 head of broccoli with stem

2 medium carrots

1 red bell pepper

1 yellow bell pepper

2 tablespoons toasted sesame oil

¼ cup soy sauce

1 tablespoon sesame seeds

1 tablespoon chopped fresh parsley

INSTRUCTIONS:

1. Cut the chicken breasts into cubes. Place the cubes in a baking dish, add 1 tablespoon of olive oil and the ginger, cover with plastic wrap, transfer to the refrigerator and let them marinate for at least 4 hours or overnight if possible.

2. Heat a skillet over medium heat and add 1 tablespoon of olive oil. Drain the marinated chicken, add it to the pan and cook for about 10 minutes, tossing the cubes to cook on all sides until they are cooked through. Remove the chicken from the pan and shred it with two forks.

3. Meanwhile, cut off the broccoli stem from the florets. Cut off any dry ends and lightly peel the stem.

4. Trim the ends off the carrots and peel them.

5. Spiralize the broccoli stem and the carrots into thin noodles.

6. Cut the remaining broccoli into small florets and chop the red and yellow bell peppers into thin strips.

7. Add the sesame oil (or more olive oil), broccoli florets, broccoli noodles, carrot noodles and peppers to the pan and cook over high heat for about 10 minutes, stirring occasionally.

8. In the last 2 minutes, add the soy sauce and the cooked, shredded chicken to the pan and stir to combine and coat all the ingredients with the sauce.

9. Garnish with the sesame seeds and fresh parsley and serve.

GRILLED CHICKEN HALLOUMI KEBABS

Break out the barbecue! If you haven't tried halloumi cheese, you should do it now!
It's one of the best cheeses for grilling because it retains its shape and caramelizes
beautifully, making it perfect for Grilled Chicken Halloumi Kebabs.
You can use queso de freir if you can't find halloumi.

PREP TIME: 20 minutes
COOK TIME: 15 minutes
SERVES: 4 people

INGREDIENTS:

12 ounces chicken tenderloin

8 ounces halloumi cheese

Salt and pepper

½ teaspoon dried dill

1 recipe Cucumber Mint
   Salad *(page 38)*

INSTRUCTIONS:

1. Preheat your grill to about 400°F. If you're using wooden
   skewers, be sure to soak them in water to prevent them from
   catching fire while grilling.

2. Cube the chicken tenderloin and halloumi cheese so that
   they are similar sizes, about 1-inch cubes.

3. Season the chicken with the salt, pepper and dried dill and
   toss to coat the chicken with the spices.

4. Thread the skewers, alternating the chicken and halloumi
   cubes, and grill them for about 15 minutes, flipping once.
   The cook time may vary based on your grill.

5. Serve the Grilled Chicken Halloumi Kebabs hot on top of
   the Cucumber Mint Salad.

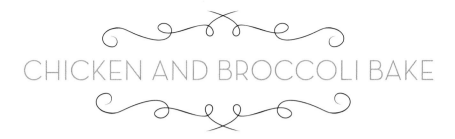

CHICKEN AND BROCCOLI BAKE

Need dinner for the week? Look no further than Chicken and Broccoli Bake with white cheddar. It's super easy to make and you can probably find each ingredient in your fridge right now.

PREP TIME: 10 minutes
COOK TIME: 50 minutes
SERVES: 4 people

INGREDIENTS:

3 tablespoons olive oil

4 broccoli stems

1 head of broccoli

12 ounces boneless, skinless chicken breasts

2 tablespoons unsalted butter

½ medium white onion, chopped

½ cup heavy cream

2 teaspoons Dijon mustard

Salt and pepper

10 ounces sharp white cheddar cheese, shredded

Chopped fresh parsley, for garnish

INSTRUCTIONS:

1. Preheat the oven to 350°F. Grease a 13 x 9-inch casserole dish with 1 tablespoon of the olive oil.

2. Trim the ends off the broccoli stems and peel them. Spiralize them into thick noodles.

3. Chop the head of broccoli into florets.

4. On a clean surface, pound the chicken breasts with a meat tenderizer or rolling pin until they're about ½ inch thick.

5. Heat 2 tablespoons of olive oil in a large skillet over medium heat. Sauté the chicken breasts for 5 to 7 minutes on each side or until the juices run clear when cut. Shred the chicken with two forks and set aside.

6. In the same pan, melt the butter and then add the chopped onion and broccoli florets. Sauté for 2 minutes and then add the heavy cream. Stir the cream continuously and add the Dijon mustard, salt and pepper to taste.

7. Once thickened, remove the sauce from the heat and stir in 8 ounces of the cheese until it fully melts.

8. Add the broccoli cheese sauce, shredded chicken and broccoli noodles to the prepared casserole dish. Stir to combine.

9. Cover the dish with foil and bake it for 20 minutes.

10. Uncover and sprinkle the remaining cheese over the top. Bake for 10 more minutes.

11. Remove the dish from the oven, garnish with the fresh parsley and serve.

CHICKEN PARMESAN ZOODLES

Did you know that grated Parmesan cheese acts as a great low-carb crust for breading chicken? Neither did we before we went low carb. Now we use it in our Chicken Parmesan Zoodles without fail!

PREP TIME: 10 minutes
COOK TIME: 20 minutes
SERVES: 4 people

INGREDIENTS:

1 pound boneless, skinless chicken breasts

2 medium eggs

½ cup grated Parmesan cheese

1 teaspoon dried basil

1 teaspoon dried oregano

1 teaspoon garlic powder

Salt and pepper

4 zucchini

1 tablespoon olive oil

4 cloves garlic, chopped

2 cups marinara sauce

2 ounces fresh mozzarella cheese

Chopped fresh basil, for garnish

INSTRUCTIONS:

1. Preheat the oven to 400°F. Line a 13 x 9-inch baking sheet with foil and grease the foil.

2. Place the chicken breasts on a clean work surface and pound them with a meat tenderizer or rolling pin until they're ½ to ¾ inch thick.

3. Crack the eggs into a large bowl and whisk them with a fork.

4. In a small bowl, combine the Parmesan cheese with the dried basil, oregano, garlic powder, salt and pepper and spread the mixture evenly on a large, shallow plate.

5. Dredge each chicken breast in the beaten eggs and then press gently into the Parmesan cheese mixture. Make sure each breast is fully coated in the "breading."

6. Place each coated breast on the prepared baking sheet and bake for 20 minutes.

7. Meanwhile, trim the ends off the zucchini and spiralize them into thin noodles.

8. Heat the olive oil in a pan over medium heat. Add the chopped garlic and cook for 3 minutes, then add the noodles and cook them for 2 minutes, tossing continuously.

9. Add 1 cup of the marinara sauce and let it simmer for 5 minutes.

10. Slice the fresh mozzarella into as many pieces as you have chicken.

11. When the chicken has 5 minutes remaining, take the baking sheet out and add the fresh mozzarella slices to each chicken breast, and then ladle the remaining 1 cup of marinara evenly over the top of each chicken breast. Put the chicken breasts back into the oven to finish cooking.

12. Serve the chicken on top of the zoodles and garnish with the fresh basil leaves.

CHICKEN CACCIATORE
WITH CACIO E PEPE

This robust, Italian-inspired sauce brings out the simple, creamy flavor of our Chicken Cacciatore with Cacio e Pepe. Cut the carbs by grilling the chicken instead of breading it and let the flavors of the sauce shine through.

PREP TIME: 15 minutes
COOK TIME: 30 minutes
SERVES: 4 people

INGREDIENTS:

24 ounces boneless, skinless chicken breasts

Salt and pepper

1 tablespoon olive oil

1 white onion, chopped

1 green bell pepper, chopped

2 cloves garlic, sliced

1 14.5 ounce can diced tomatoes

¼ cup tomato paste

8 ounces mushrooms, sliced

2 tablespoons capers

1 teaspoon dried basil

1 teaspoon dried oregano

½ teaspoon dried thyme

1 recipe Cacio e Pepe
(page 150)

INSTRUCTIONS:

1. Preheat your grill to about 500°F. Season the chicken breasts with salt and pepper and sear for about 3 minutes on each side.

2. Heat the olive oil in a large pan over medium heat and cook the white onion and green bell pepper until softened, 6 to 8 minutes.

3. Add the garlic, diced tomatoes and tomato paste. Stir everything with a wooden spoon until combined.

4. Let this come to a simmer and then add the mushrooms, capers, basil, oregano, thyme and salt and pepper to taste. Allow this to simmer while the chicken finishes searing.

5. Add the seared chicken breasts to the simmering sauce and let them cook for an additional 20 minutes.

6. Serve the chicken on top of the Cacio e Pepe with a heaping serving of the sauce the chicken was simmered in.

TARRAGON CHICKEN AND BROCCOLI

An impressive dinner doesn't have to have a million ingredients. Tarragon Chicken and Broccoli can be thrown together with fewer than ten ingredients and puts an interesting twist on broccoli by adding a slightly sweet, creamy sauce.

PREP TIME: 10 minutes
COOK TIME: 20 minutes
SERVES: 4 people

INGREDIENTS:

4 (4-ounce) boneless, skinless chicken thighs

Salt and pepper

2 tablespoons olive oil

4 large broccoli heads with the stems

Sauce

1 tablespoon olive oil

½ white onion, chopped

1 cup sour cream

1 teaspoon dried tarragon

Salt and pepper

INSTRUCTIONS:

1. On a clean surface, pound the chicken thighs with a meat tenderizer or rolling pin until they're about ½ inch thick. Season both sides of the chicken with salt and pepper.

2. Heat 1 tablespoon of the olive oil in a large pan over medium heat. Sauté the chicken thighs for about 4 minutes on each side, until almost fully cooked. Set the thighs aside on a plate to rest while you prepare the sauce.

3. To make the sauce, heat olive oil in a skillet over medium heat. Add the onion and cook until it turns translucent, 5 to 6 minutes. Lower the heat and add the sour cream and tarragon. Add salt and pepper to taste. Stir to combine and let it simmer for about 2 minutes.

4. Add the chicken thighs to the pan with the sauce and cook for about 10 minutes, flipping a few times.

5. Meanwhile, separate the broccoli heads from the stems, trimming off any dry ends. Spiralize the stems into ribbons.

6. Heat the remaining 1 tablespoon of olive oil in a skillet, add the noodles and about 2 cups of the broccoli florets, season with salt and pepper and cook for about 5 minutes, tossing continuously. The noodles should soften and the florets should turn a brighter green with the edges slightly brown.

7. Serve the creamy tarragon chicken thighs on top of the cooked broccoli noodles. Add a few broccoli florets to each plate as well.

CHICKEN PAD THAI

Here's a fun recipe to try out if you're feeling like making some authentic Asian food. The texture of scrambled eggs in stir-fries is always fun and the peanuts give everything a good crunch. The fact that this Chicken Pad Thai is low carb is a bonus, too!

PREP TIME: **15** minutes
COOK TIME: **15** minutes
SERVES: **4** people

INGREDIENTS:

1 tablespoon olive oil

1 white onion, roughly chopped

2 cloves garlic, minced

1 pound boneless, skinless chicken thighs

Salt and pepper

2 zucchini

1 large egg

2 tablespoons soy sauce

½ teaspoon red pepper flakes (optional)

1 ounce peanuts, crushed or whole

1 lime, cut into wedges

INSTRUCTIONS:

1. Heat the olive oil in a wok or large pan over medium heat, add the chopped onion and cook until it is translucent, 5 to 6 minutes. Add the garlic and cook until it is fragrant, about 3 minutes.

2. Season the chicken thighs with salt and pepper and place them in the wok. Let them cook for 5 to 7 minutes on each side, or until fully cooked.

3. Remove the chicken thighs from the wok and shred them using two forks.

4. Trim the ends off the zucchini and spiralize them into thin noodles. Set the noodles aside.

5. Create a well in the center of the wok and crack an egg into it. Allow it to cook for a few seconds and then scramble it into large chunks.

6. Add the zucchini noodles to the pan. Let the noodles cook for just about 2 minutes, tossing continuously.

7. Add the shredded chicken and finish it all off with the soy sauce, a squeeze of lime, and red pepper flakes, if using.

8. Top the Chicken Pad Thai with the peanuts and serve with the lime wedges alongside the dish.

MEDITERRANEAN CHICKEN ZOODLE SALAD

Mediterranean salads are always refreshing, and our Mediterranean Chicken Zoodle Salad is no different. Citrus, olives, capers and feta bring some of the best flavors to this delicious summer salad.

PREP TIME: **15 minutes**
COOK TIME: **15 minutes**
SERVES: **4 people**

INGREDIENTS:

12 ounces boneless, skinless chicken breasts

4 tablespoons olive oil

4 Campari tomatoes, diced

½ medium white onion, diced

Juice of 1 lemon

2 ounces pitted olives

1 ounce capers

2 medium cucumbers

2 medium zucchini

4 ounces feta cheese

Chopped fresh parsley, for garnish

INSTRUCTIONS:

1. Place the chicken breasts on a clean work surface and pound them with a meat tenderizer or rolling pin until they're about ½ inch thick.

2. Heat 2 tablespoons of the olive oil in a large pan over medium heat and sauté the chicken breasts for 5 to 7 minutes on each side or until golden on the outside and the juices run clear when cut.

3. Meanwhile, add the diced tomatoes and onion to a large mixing bowl along with the lemon juice, olives, capers and remaining 2 tablespoons of olive oil.

4. Trim the ends off the cucumbers, peel them and spiralize them into thick noodles. Add the noodles to the mixing bowl.

5. Remove the chicken from the pan and shred it using two forks. Add the shredded chicken to the mixing bowl.

6. Trim the ends off the zucchini and spiralize them into thick noodles.

7. Lightly cook the zoodles in the same pan for 2 minutes and then add them to the mixing bowl.

8. Crumble the feta cheese into the mixing bowl and toss the ingredients well.

9. Garnish the salad with the fresh parsley and serve.

CHICKEN PAPRIKASH
WITH SQUASH NOODLES

Creamy, well-seasoned Chicken Paprikash with Squash Noodles has Hungarian origins and couldn't be simpler to make. It looks beautiful and the recipe could easily be doubled to please a crowd. We like to eat it right from the cast-iron skillet we prepared it in!

PREP TIME: 10 minutes
COOK TIME: 25 minutes
SERVES: 4 people

INGREDIENTS:

2 tablespoons olive oil

½ medium white onion, diced

4 cloves garlic, minced

2 teaspoons paprika

Salt and pepper

2 Roma tomatoes, diced

1 medium red bell pepper, diced

1 cup chicken broth

1 pound boneless, skinless chicken thighs

2 large yellow squash

¼ cup heavy cream

INSTRUCTIONS:

1. Heat 1 tablespoon of the olive oil in a cast-iron skillet over medium heat. Add the onion and cook until it is translucent, about 5 minutes. Add the garlic and cook for 2 minutes.

2. Add the paprika and season with salt and pepper. Mix everything until the onion and garlic are fully coated in paprika.

3. Stir in the tomatoes, bell pepper and chicken broth.

4. Raise the heat to bring the chicken broth to a boil quickly and then reduce the heat and allow everything to simmer for about 15 minutes.

5. In the meantime, place the chicken thighs on a clean work surface and pound them with a meat tenderizer or rolling pin until they're about ½ inch thick.

6. Heat the remaining tablespoon of oil in a large pan over medium-high heat. Sauté the chicken thighs for 5 to 7 minutes on each side or until golden and firm to the touch. Remove the chicken thighs from the pan and shred them with two forks.

7. Trim the ends off the squash. Spiralize into thick noodles.

8. Add the shredded chicken, heavy cream, squash noodles and more salt and pepper (if necessary) to the sauce and cook for another 5 minutes. Serve.

YELLOW SQUASH BEEF BOLOGNESE

Saucy yellow squash noodles taste and feel just like traditional pasta. Add a bit of ground beef and you get a good Bolognese sauce to pair them with!

PREP TIME: 15 minutes
COOK TIME: 30 minutes
SERVES: 4 people

INGREDIENTS:

2 tablespoons olive oil

1 pound 85% lean ground beef

4 cloves garlic, minced

1 teaspoon dried oregano

1 teaspoon red pepper flakes

1 cup dry red wine

4 Roma tomatoes, diced

Salt and pepper

2 large yellow squash

1 teaspoon dried basil

¼ cup heavy cream

½ cup grated Parmesan cheese

Chopped fresh basil, for garnish

INSTRUCTIONS:

1. Heat the olive oil in a large skillet over medium heat, add the ground beef and fry for 5 to 7 minutes, until it starts to brown.

2. Add the minced garlic, dried oregano and red pepper flakes and cook for another 2 minutes.

3. Pour the red wine into the pan, add the tomatoes and salt and pepper to taste and stir until everything is combined well.

4. Bring the sauce to a boil, then lower the heat and let it simmer for about 10 minutes.

5. Meanwhile, trim the ends off the yellow squash and spiralize them into thick noodles.

6. Add the dried basil and heavy cream to the sauce, stir and allow everything to simmer for an additional 10 minutes.

7. In the last 3 minutes of cooking, add the yellow squash noodles to the pan and let them cook and soften.

8. Divide the squash and sauce into equal portions, top with the grated Parmesan and fresh basil and serve.

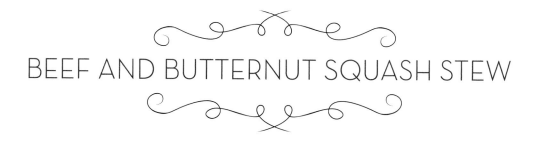

BEEF AND BUTTERNUT SQUASH STEW

Cooler months in the fall beg for this warm, hearty Beef and Butternut Squash Stew. It just so happens that autumn bears the most delicious squash, so eat it all up!

PREP TIME: **15 minutes**
COOK TIME: **3 minutes**
SERVES: **4–6 people**

INGREDIENTS:

3 tablespoons olive oil

1 medium yellow onion, chopped

4 cloves garlic, chopped

2 pounds beef sirloin steak

Salt and pepper

1 cup dry red wine (we use a Cabernet Sauvignon)

1 large butternut squash

2 Roma tomatoes, chopped

1 sprig fresh rosemary

2 cups beef broth

2 cups water

Chopped fresh parsley, for garnish

INSTRUCTIONS:

1. Heat the olive oil in a large soup pot over medium heat. Add the onion and garlic and cook until the onion is translucent, about 5 minutes.

2. Cut the beef into 2-inch cubes and season them liberally with salt. Add the cubes to the pot and cook them for about 5 minutes, or until they are brown on all sides.

3. Add the red wine to the pot and stir all the contents with a wooden spoon, gently scraping the bottom to get off all of the caramelized bits.

4. Cut off the bulbous half of the butternut squash. Cut the end of the straighter half off and peel its hard skin multiple times until you reach the bright orange inside. Spiralize the squash into ribbons.

5. Add the butternut ribbons, chopped tomatoes, rosemary, beef broth and water to the pot. Season with salt and pepper to taste.

6. Bring the stew to a boil over high heat and then decrease the heat to low. Cover the pot and let it simmer for 2 to 3 hours. The beef should be fork tender and falling apart easily.

7. Garnish with the chopped fresh parsley and serve.

BEEF STROGANOFF WITH YELLOW SQUASH RIBBONS

We love turning classic favorites into low-carb dishes! Beef Stroganoff is popular in the Russian community for its creaminess that you don't find in many Russian dishes. Bursting with flavor from the juicy steak and mushrooms, it's impossible not to love our Beef Stroganoff with Yellow Squash Ribbons!

PREP TIME: 15 minutes
COOK TIME: 40 minutes
SERVES: 4 people

INGREDIENTS:

1 pound beef top sirloin

2 tablespoons olive oil

2 tablespoons butter

1 pound mushrooms, sliced

½ medium white onion, diced

4 cloves garlic, minced

1 cup beef broth

2 large yellow squash

¼ cup sour cream

Salt and pepper

Fresh parsley, for garnish

INSTRUCTIONS:

1. Cut the sirloin steak into thin tips about 1 inch long and ½ inch thick.

2. Heat the olive oil in a large skillet over high heat, add the sirloin tips and brown on both sides, about 5-8 minutes. Remove the steak from the pan and place on a plate.

3. Decrease the heat to medium and add the butter and sliced mushrooms to the pan. Scrape up any bits of steak that may be stuck to the skillet with a wooden spoon.

4. After 5 minutes, you should see the mushrooms shrivel a bit and brown. Add the onion and garlic to the pan and cook until the onion turns translucent, about 5 minutes.

5. Pour in the beef broth and add the steak back to the pan. Cover the pan and let everything simmer for about 30 minutes over low heat.

6. Trim the ends off the yellow squash, spiralize them into ribbons and add the noodles along with the sour cream to the pan. Cook, uncovered, for an additional 10 minutes.

7. Season with salt and pepper to taste and stir everything one last time.

8. Divide Stroganoff into equal portions and garnish with the fresh parsley.

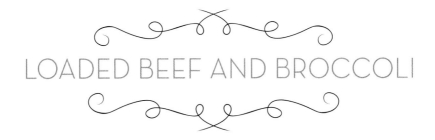

LOADED BEEF AND BROCCOLI

Who wants boring beef and broccoli? Make a batch of our Loaded Beef and Broccoli to have on hand for the week and enjoy tons of flavor for dinner and even have leftovers for lunch! Perfect for work or school—just reheat and eat!

PREP TIME: 5 minutes
COOK TIME: 20 minutes
SERVES: 4 people

INGREDIENTS:

24 ounces 85% lean ground beef

Salt and pepper

4 cloves garlic

2 large eggs, beaten

2 heads broccoli with stems

4 ounces shredded pepper jack cheese

1 teaspoon sesame seeds

½ teaspoon red pepper flakes

INSTRUCTIONS:

1. Add the ground beef to a large pan over medium-high heat and cook, breaking it up into smaller pieces with a wooden spoon. Season the meat with salt and pepper to taste.

2. Use a garlic press to squeeze the garlic into the pan while the beef is browning and let it cook with the beef for 5 minutes.

3. Add the beaten eggs to the pan and keep stirring so the eggs combine with the beef. Decrease the heat to low and let everything simmer for 10 minutes.

4. In the meantime, cut the stems off the heads of broccoli, peel them and spiralize them into thick noodles.

5. Chop the remaining broccoli into smaller florets and add them, along with the broccoli noodles, to the pan. Cover and let everything cook for 10 minutes.

6. In the last 3 minutes, add the shredded pepper jack cheese and stir all the contents in the pan to let the cheese melt evenly.

7. Garnish with the sesame seeds and red pepper flakes and serve.

SPICY CASHEW BEEF

Spicy Cashew Beef was inspired by a Thai dish we enjoyed. It was full of perfectly cooked onion, carrots and zucchini, plus fun roasted cashews. Something about the combination of creamy, spicy and crunchy makes this the perfect dinner.

PREP TIME: 20 minutes
COOK TIME: 20 minutes
SERVES: 4 people

INGREDIENTS:

2 medium zucchini

2 medium carrots

2 tablespoons olive oil

½ red onion, diced

2 cloves garlic, minced

1-inch cube fresh ginger, grated

1 fresh jalapeño, sliced (optional)

1 teaspoon red pepper flakes (optional)

Salt and pepper

20 ounces sirloin steak

¼ cup beef broth

2 tablespoons heavy cream

3 ounces roasted cashews, whole or chopped

Scallions, chopped, for garnish

INSTRUCTIONS:

1. Trim the ends off the zucchini and carrots. Peel the carrots and spiralize both the carrots and the zucchini into thick noodles.

2. Add 1 tablespoon of the olive oil to a wok or deep skillet over medium heat and cook the onion, garlic, ginger and carrots for about 5 minutes.

3. Add the zucchini noodles, jalapeño (if using), red pepper flakes (if using), and salt and pepper to taste and cook for 2 more minutes. Set everything aside on a plate while you prepare the rest of the recipe.

4. Slice the sirloin steak into strips about ½ inch thick and 1 inch wide. Add them to the same skillet along with the remaining 1 tablespoon of olive oil and cook over medium heat until browned on all sides, about 5 minutes.

5. Add the veggies back to the pan and toss everything well to combine.

6. Pour in the beef broth and heavy cream and allow everything to cook, uncovered, for about 8 minutes. Much of the liquid should be evaporated.

7. Divide the beef and noodles into equal portions and sprinkle with the roasted cashews and chopped scallion. Serve.

BEEF LO MEIN

When you remove the carb-y noodles from the traditional lo mein, the result is a vegetable-
and nutrient-packed meal that is so good, you won't even notice their absence.
Our Beef Lo Mein is super flavorful and completely good for you.

PREP TIME: 5 minutes
COOK TIME: 20 minutes
SERVES: 6–8 people

INGREDIENTS:

1 tablespoon sesame oil, or
    more as needed

1 pound flank steak

8 ounces mushrooms, sliced

1 red bell pepper, diced

1 medium carrot

2 yellow squash

2 tablespoons soy sauce

1 cup whole snap peas

Salt and pepper

INSTRUCTIONS:

1. Heat the sesame oil in a very large pan over high heat, add
   the flank steak and cook for about 5 minutes on each side.
   Let it rest on a plate for 10 minutes before slicing it.

2. In the leftover sesame oil, cook the mushrooms and diced
   red bell pepper until slightly browned. Add a bit more
   sesame oil if necessary.

3. Trim the ends off the carrot and yellow squash. Peel the
   carrot, spiralize the carrot and the squash into thin
   noodles and add them to the pan. Toss the noodles to
   coat them well.

4. Add the soy sauce to the pan and let the noodles cook for
   about 3 minutes.

5. Slice the flank steak into thin strips and add it to the pan.

6. Add the snap peas and season everything with salt and
   pepper. Let the flank steak and snap peas cook for about
   2 minutes just to warm up.

7. Mix everything well with tongs and divide into equal
   portions.

CHIMICHURRI SKIRT STEAK WITH BROCCOLI SLAW

Bold doesn't begin to describe this Chimichurri Skirt Steak with Broccoli Slaw—it is a garlic lover's dream! Cilantro may not be for everyone, but we give it credit for the unbeatable taste of this recipe. Broccoli slaw pairs well with the bold flavors and acts as a mid-meal refresher.

PREP TIME: **20 minutes**
COOK TIME: **12 minutes**
SERVES: **4 people**

INGREDIENTS:

Sauce

½ cup finely minced fresh cilantro

¼ cup finely minced fresh parsley

4 cloves garlic, sliced

1 shallot, minced

2 tablespoons white vinegar

¾ cup olive oil

1 teaspoon salt

Steak

1 pound skirt steak

1 teaspoon salt

½ teaspoon pepper

½ teaspoon garlic powder

1 tablespoon olive oil

Broccoli Slaw

2 broccoli stems

1 medium carrot

½ head of white cabbage

½ cup mayonnaise

Juice of ½ lemon

Salt and pepper

INSTRUCTIONS:

1. To make the sauce, combine all the sauce ingredients in a bowl and stir well. Chill it in the fridge until ready to serve.

2. To make the steak, season the skirt steak with the salt, pepper and garlic powder. Heat the olive oil in a pan over high heat, let the pan get very hot, add the steak and cook it for 6 minutes on each side until it's just slightly pink in the center when cut. Let the steak rest on a plate for 10 minutes before cutting it.

3. To make the broccoli slaw, trim the ends off the broccoli stems and carrots and peel them. Spiralize them both into ribbons and shred the cabbage.

4. Add all the vegetables to a deep mixing bowl and dress with the mayonnaise, lemon juice, salt and pepper.

5. Slice the skirt steak into ½- to 1-inch-thick pieces and serve them on top of a bed of the broccoli slaw.

6. Generously dollop each serving with the chilled chimichurri sauce and serve.

THAI-CARROT NOODLES AND STEAK

If you've never experienced cooking with peanut butter, you should try it! Warm peanut butter, crunchy or creamy, works really well with spicy and savory steak. Try Thai-Carrot Noodles and Steak and enjoy your peanut butter for dinner.

PREP TIME: 1 hour
COOK TIME: 25 minutes
SERVES: 4 people

INGREDIENTS:

1 tablespoon olive oil

24 ounces skirt steak

Salt and pepper

Chopped fresh cilantro, for garnish

Whole or chopped peanuts, for garnish

Peanut Sauce

¼ cup peanut butter

2 tablespoons soy sauce

2 cloves garlic, minced

2 tablespoons lime juice

½ -inch cube ginger

Carrot Noodles

4 medium carrots

2 tablespoons olive oil

½ medium red onion, sliced

¼ cup water

INSTRUCTIONS:

1. Season the steak with salt and pepper 1 hour before cooking.

2. Heat a large skillet over medium-high heat with the olive oil, add the steak and cook for 6 to 8 minutes on each side or until slightly pink in the center. Let it rest on a plate for about 5 minutes before slicing it.

3. To make the sauce, melt the peanut butter in a small pan over medium heat and cook for 3 to 5 minutes.

4. Meanwhile, pureé the other sauce ingredients in a food processor.

5. Stir the pureed ingredients in with the melted peanut butter. Remove the pan from the heat.

6. Peel, trim, and spiralize the carrots into noodles.

7. Heat the olive oil in a large pan over medium-high heat. Add the red onion and cook for 3 minutes, until softened.

8. Add the carrots and water. Cover and steam for 3 minutes.

9. Thinly slice the steak and add the slices to the same pan.

10. Pour the peanut sauce into the pan and mix everything together.

11. Divide the steak and noodles among 4 plates, garnish with the cilantro and peanuts and serve.

SKIRT STEAK ON HOLLANDAISE BROCCOLI NOODLES

Hollandaise isn't just for eggs Benedict! It's a great sauce to have on hand for hearty dinners with steak. Steaks love thick, salty sauces that complement their flavor. Our Skirt Steak on Hollandaise Broccoli Noodles can rival any steakhouse dish!

PREP TIME: 15 minutes
COOK TIME: 45 minutes
SERVES: 4–6 people

INGREDIENTS:

24 ounces skirt steak

Salt and pepper

2 tablespoons olive oil

4 broccoli stems

Hollandaise Sauce

3 egg yolks

1 tablespoon fresh lemon juice

8 tablespoons (½ cup or 1 stick) unsalted butter, cold

¼ teaspoon cayenne

Salt and pepper

INSTRUCTIONS:

1. Season the skirt steak generously with salt and pepper.

2. Heat the olive oil in a 12-inch cast-iron skillet over high heat, let the pan get hot, add the steak and cook for 7 minutes on each side. The steak should be browned and slightly pink in the center when cut. Remove it from the pan and let it rest on a plate for 10 minutes before slicing it.

3. Meanwhile, trim any dry ends off the broccoli stems, peel them and spiralize them into thick noodles.

4. Add the broccoli noodles to the same pan and let them cook for about 5 minutes, tossing continuously.

5. To make the Hollandaise sauce, whisk the egg yolks in a double boiler over simmering water. If you don't have a double boiler, try fitting a metal bowl over a pot of simmering water or simply use a small pan over very low heat. Whisk until the egg yolks have slightly thickened. Add the lemon juice and whisk to incorporate it.

6. Continue to whisk the yolks while adding 1 tablespoon of the butter at a time, whisking until each tablespoon is combined into the sauce.

7. Season the Hollandaise sauce with the cayenne and salt and pepper to taste. If the sauce is too thick, add a teaspoon of water at a time until it's the right consistency (it should be pourable, yet thick).

8. Divide the broccoli noodles among 4 to 6 serving plates and drizzle the Hollandaise sauce over the top. Slice the steak into thin pieces, place equal portions on top of the Hollandaise-covered broccoli noodles and serve.

STEAK FAJITA ZOODLES

Zoodles are so versatile! You can add almost any set of ingredients to them and have a fun dinner that's both easy to make and good for you. Succulent steak and bright peppers liven up our Steak Fajita Zoodles.

PREP TIME: 10 minutes
COOK TIME: 20 minutes
SERVES: 4 people

INGREDIENTS:

1 pound skirt steak

Salt and pepper

1 tablespoon olive oil

1 white onion, roughly chopped

1 red bell pepper, sliced

1 yellow bell pepper, sliced

2 large zucchini

Juice of 1 lime

Sriracha or Tabasco sauce (optional)

½ cup shredded pepper jack cheese

Chopped fresh cilantro, for garnish

INSTRUCTIONS:

1. Season the skirt steak liberally with salt and pepper on both sides.

2. Heat the olive oil in a very hot pan over high heat, add the steak and cook for 6 to 8 minutes on each side or until it's browned and slightly pink in the center when cut. Remove the steak from the pan and let it rest on a plate for about 10 minutes before slicing it.

3. In the same pan, cook the chopped onion until it is translucent, about 5 minutes.

4. Add the sliced red and yellow bell peppers, cover the pan and cook them for about 5 minutes, or until softened.

5. Meanwhile, trim the ends off the zucchini and spiralize them into thin or thick noodles according to your preference.

6. Slice the skirt steak into thin strips and add it and the zoodles to the pan. Season again with salt and pepper to taste and toss everything continuously for about 3 minutes.

7. Divide the Steak Fajita Zoodles into equal portions and squeeze some lime juice onto each serving.

8. Drizzle with the hot sauce, if using, and sprinkle with the pepper jack cheese and fresh cilantro.

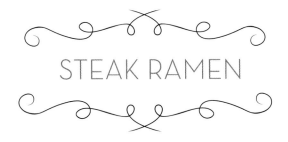

STEAK RAMEN

Ramen is traditionally served with a soft-boiled egg on top. We love the soft, creamy consistency of the egg, paired with meaty portobello mushrooms and the delicate flavors of soy sauce and honey. Our Steak Ramen is the perfect soup for a cold and blustery day.

PREP TIME: **15 minutes**
COOK TIME: **35 minutes**
SERVES: **4 people**

INGREDIENTS:

10 ounces skirt steak

2 tablespoons olive oil

½ white onion, chopped

1 red bell pepper, chopped

2 cloves garlic

1 quart chicken broth

2 portobello mushroom caps

¼ cup soy sauce

2 tablespoons honey

4 large eggs

1 daikon radish

Salt and pepper

Juice of 1 lemon

INSTRUCTIONS:

1. Heat 1 tablespoon of the oil in a skillet until it gets hot. Sear the steak for about 1 minute on each side. Let the steak rest on a plate before slicing it.

2. Add 1 tablespoon of oil to a large soup pot over medium heat. Add the onion and bell pepper and cook until the onion is translucent, about 5 minutes.

3. Add the garlic and cook for another 5 minutes.

4. Pour in the chicken broth and bring the soup to a boil.

5. Slice the portobello mushroom caps into ½-inch-thick pieces and add them to the boiling soup.

6. Lower the heat to a simmer and add the soy sauce and honey.

7. Add the 4 whole eggs (in their shells). Cook for 8 minutes. Remove them with tongs to cool down.

8. Trim the ends off the daikon radish and peel the outer skin. Spiralize it into thin noodles and add it to the simmering soup.

9. Slice the skirt steak into ½-inch-thick pieces and add them to the soup.

10. Season the soup with salt and pepper and let it simmer for about 10 minutes.

11. Divide the soup into bowls with a squeeze of lemon in each.

12. Peel the eggs and slice them in half lengthwise. Add 2 egg halves to each bowl and serve.

BALSAMIC THYME STEAK ON SPINACH PARSNIP NOODLES

A steak doesn't need much work beyond a good salting, but if you're ready for some flavor variations, we recommend balsamic vinegar and fresh thyme! The combo is great, especially when paired with a slightly sweet bed of spinach parsnip noodles.

PREP TIME: **15 minutes**
COOK TIME: **15 minutes**
SERVES: **4 people**

INGREDIENTS:

Steak

24 ounces flank steak

¼ cup balsamic vinegar

¼ cup olive oil

10 sprigs fresh thyme

1 teaspoon salt

½ teaspoon pepper

Noodles

1 tablespoon olive oil

12 ounces spinach

2 large parsnips

Salt and pepper

INSTRUCTIONS:

1. To make the steak, marinate the flank steak ahead of time to ensure a softer, juicier result. Whisk together vinegar, oil, thyme, salt, and pepper in a baking dish. Submerge steak and let sit in refrigerator for at least 4 hours.

2. When ready to cook, preheat the oven to the broil setting with a 12-inch cast-iron skillet or other large oven-safe pan inside.

3. After about 10 minutes, take the cast-iron skillet out of the oven with an oven mitt and place it on the stove.

4. Let the steak sear for 30 seconds on each side.

5. Transfer skillet back to oven and broil for 5 minutes on each side. Remove and set aside, covered, for 10 minutes.

6. To make the noodles, heat the olive oil in a large frying pan over medium heat, add the spinach and let it wilt.

7. Trim the ends off the parsnips and peel them. Spiralize them into thin noodles and add them to the pan. Toss the parsnip noodles to coat them in the olive oil and wilted spinach. Season with salt and pepper.

8. Lower the heat, cover the noodles and let them cook for about 8 minutes, or until softened.

9. Slice the steak against the grain of the meat into thin slices.

10. Divide the noodles into equal portions and top with the sliced flank steak.

DRUNKEN PARSNIP NOODLES WITH SIRLOIN STEAK

Thai cuisine uses basil in abundance. Drunken Parsnip Noodles are heavy on the basil and flavor! You get sweet, savory, spicy and salty all in one dish and with only a fraction of the carbs found in traditional drunken noodles!

PREP TIME: 10 minutes
COOK TIME: 20 minutes
SERVES: 4 people

INGREDIENTS:

2 large parsnips

1 ounce fresh basil, plus more for garnish

1 tablespoon sesame or olive oil

12 ounces sirloin steak

½ white onion, chopped

4 cloves garlic, chopped

1-inch cube ginger, grated

2 medium carrots

1 medium zucchini

2 tablespoons soy sauce

Salt and black pepper

2 scallions, chopped

½ teaspoon red pepper flakes (optional)

INSTRUCTIONS:

1. Bring a pot of lightly salted water to a boil over medium-high heat.

2. Trim the ends off the parsnips and peel them. Spiralize them into thick noodles. Add the noodles to the boiling water and cook for 5 to 6 minutes, or until soft.

3. Drain the water and add the basil to the hot noodles. Stir the leaves in and allow them to wilt in the parsnips' residual heat.

4. Heat the sesame oil in a skillet or wok over high heat, add the sirloin steak and cook for 4 to 6 minutes on each side, depending on the thickness of the steak. The steak should be brown on the outside and slightly pink in the center when cut. Remove the steak from the pan and let it rest on a plate before slicing it.

5. Lower the heat, add the white onion to the same pan and cook until it is translucent, about 5 minutes. Add the chopped garlic and grated ginger and let it all cook until fragrant, about 3 minutes.

6. Chop the carrots into ¼-inch-thick rounds, add them to the pan and cook them until they're a bit soft, about 5-6 minutes.

7. Slice the zucchini into thick sticks, add them to the pan and cook until they are soft and slightly browned, about 4-5 minutes.

8. Slice the cooked steak and add it back to the pan along with the soy sauce. Season with salt and pepper and toss to combine. Let it all cook for just about a minute.

9. Add the parsnip noodles and toss to combine. Divide the mixture among 4 plates and top with more fresh basil, chopped scallion and red pepper flakes, if using.

GRILLED SAUSAGES WITH
HONEY-GLAZED BUTTERNUT NOODLES

Grilled Sausages with Honey-Glazed Butternut Noodles are a favorite of ours in the summer!
Butternut squash noodles have a natural sweetness, and combined with honey, that
sweetness really shines. They are the perfect accompaniment to savory sausages
fresh off the grill. It's a great combo you'll enjoy over and over.

PREP TIME: **15 minutes**
COOK TIME: **15 minutes**
SERVES: **4 people**

INGREDIENTS:

1 large butternut squash

12 (1-ounce) pork sausage
links, cooked

2 tablespoons olive oil

1 small white onion, diced

4 ounces fresh kale

Salt

2 tablespoons honey

INSTRUCTIONS:

1. Preheat a grill to about 400°F.

2. Cut off the bulbous half of the butternut squash. Cut the end of the straighter half off and peel its hard skin multiple times until you reach the bright orange inside. Spiralize the squash into thick noodles.

3. Make a few slices into each sausage link on one side about a quarter of the way in. Grill them for about 10 minutes, flipping them halfway through.

4. Heat the oil in a large pan over medium heat, add the onion and cook until the onion is translucent, about 5 minutes.

5. Add the butternut noodles and kale and cook them for 10 minutes. Season everything with salt to taste.

6. On a serving platter, make a bed out of the butternut noodles, kale and onions and drizzle with the honey. Add the sausage links on top and serve.

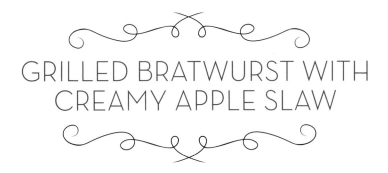

GRILLED BRATWURST WITH CREAMY APPLE SLAW

Start up your grill this summer for a delicious German lunch! The robust flavors of grilled bratwurst are the perfect pairing for our sweet, spiralized Creamy Apple Slaw.

PREP TIME: **10 minutes**
COOK TIME: **20 minutes**
SERVES: **4-6 people**

INGREDIENTS:

8-12 bratwurst sausages

1 recipe Creamy Apple Slaw
(*page 157*)

German mustard, for serving

INSTRUCTIONS:

1. Preheat a grill to about 400°F.

2. Grill the bratwurst sausages for 8 to 10 minutes on each side, making sure not to move them too much in order to get nice grill marks.

3. Divide the Creamy Apple Slaw among 4 to 6 plates.

4. Place 2 grilled bratwurst sausages atop each bed of slaw.

5. Add a drizzle of German mustard to each bratwurst and serve.

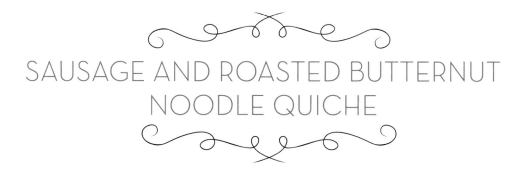

SAUSAGE AND ROASTED BUTTERNUT NOODLE QUICHE

A quiche is a great way to use up lots of eggs and vegetables. Quiche is versatile and quick to make and can feed a crowd. You can adjust the recipe to feed more or fewer people and throw in their favorite ingredients as well, like peppers, spinach and even olives!

PREP TIME: **15 minutes**
COOK TIME: **45 minutes**
SERVES: **4–6 people**

INGREDIENTS:

Crust

1 large butternut squash

4 tablespoons unsalted butter, at room temperature

1 large egg

Filling

12 ounces sweet Italian sausages

1 tablespoon olive oil

½ medium yellow onion, chopped

2 cloves garlic, minced

½ teaspoon dried basil

½ teaspoon dried oregano

8 ounces white mushrooms, sliced

10 large eggs

Salt and pepper

Fresh basil, for garnish

INSTRUCTIONS:

1. Preheat the oven to 375°F.

2. To make the crust, cut the ends off of the straighter half of the squash and peel off skin. Spiralize squash into thin noodles.

3. In a large bowl, combine the butter, egg and noodles.

4. Press the squash noodles into a 9-inch pie dish until you have an even thickness on both the bottom and the sides.

5. Transfer the dish to the oven and bake for 20 minutes.

6. In the meantime, remove the sausages from their casings.

7. Heat the olive oil in a skillet over medium heat. Cook the sausages for about 4 minutes, breaking up the meat.

8. Transfer the sausage to a bowl. Add the onion, garlic, dried basil and oregano to the pan. Cook them for about 5 minutes, or until the onion is softened.

9. Add the mushrooms and cook for another 3 minutes. Remove the pan from the heat.

10. Once crust is done, arrange the sautéed vegetables and sausage evenly on top.

11. Whisk eggs, pepper and salt in a bowl and pour over the sausage and vegetables.

12. Return quiche to oven and bake for 25 minutes. Put on a rack to cool for 5 minutes.

13. Garnish the quiche with basil, slice, and serve.

SAUCY SAUSAGE AND PEPPER ZOODLES

For a robust, hearty dinner fit to please a family, we recommend Saucy Sausages and Pepper Zoodles. Sausage and zucchini go hand in hand in many Italian dishes, especially when cooked in a sweet marinara sauce.

PREP TIME: **15 minutes**
COOK TIME: **15 minutes**
SERVES: **6–6 people**

INGREDIENTS:

2 tablespoons olive oil

1 white onion, roughly chopped

1 red bell pepper, roughly chopped

1 yellow bell pepper, roughly chopped

4 cloves garlic, roughly chopped

6 Andouille sausages, cooked

2 cups marinara sauce

2 large zucchini

Salt and pepper

Shaved Parmesan cheese, for garnish

Fresh basil leaves, for garnish

INSTRUCTIONS:

1. Heat the olive oil in a large pan over medium heat, add the onion and red and yellow peppers and cook for 6 to 8 minutes.

2. Add the chopped garlic and cook everything for about 3 minutes longer, until the garlic is fragrant.

3. Slice the Andouille sausages into ½-inch-thick pieces and add them to the pan. Let the sausages cook for about 5 minutes, just to heat them through. Add the marinara sauce, stir with a wooden spoon to combine everything and lower the heat to a simmer.

4. Meanwhile, spiralize the zucchini into thin or thick noodles according to your preference.

5. Add the noodles to the pan and make sure they are more or less submerged under the marinara sauce. Let the noodles cook for 3 to 5 minutes until they've softened.

6. Test to see if the dish needs salt and pepper and add as necessary.

7. Divide everything into equal portions and top each plate with shaved (or grated) Parmesan cheese and fresh basil leaves.

ASIAN BEEF SLAW

One-pan dinners are lifesavers when it comes to getting dinner on the table fast.
Our Asian Beef Slaw has a unique flavor but uses some pretty basic ingredients to
make sure you have an impressive dinner in no time.

PREP TIME: **10** minutes
COOK TIME: **20** minutes
SERVES: **4** people

INGREDIENTS:

1 tablespoon sesame or
    olive oil

½ white onion, chopped

2 cloves garlic, minced

1-inch cube ginger, grated

1 pound ground beef

10 ounces cabbage

1 large carrot

2 tablespoons soy sauce

1 tablespoon hot sauce
    (optional)

Salt and pepper

1 teaspoon sesame seeds

2 scallions, chopped

INSTRUCTIONS:

1. Heat the sesame oil in a large pan or wok over medium heat.
   Add the chopped onion and cook until it is translucent,
   about 6 minutes, then add the garlic and ginger and cook
   until they are fragrant, about 3 minutes.

2. Add the ground beef to the pan and cook until it's browned,
   breaking it up into small pieces with a wooden spoon.

3. Meanwhile, using the ribbon attachment on your spiralizer,
   shred the cabbage.

4. Trim the ends off the carrot and peel it. Spiralize it into thin
   noodles.

5. Add the cabbage, carrot, soy sauce and hot sauce, if using, to
   the pan. Season the ingredients with salt and pepper and stir
   to combine well.

6. Cook, uncovered, for about 10 minutes, stirring occasionally.

7. To serve, garnish the Asian Beef Slaw with the sesame seeds
   and chopped scallion.

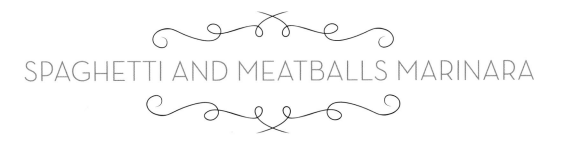

SPAGHETTI AND MEATBALLS MARINARA

If you need to persuade your kids to try yellow squash in place of carb-y, glutinous noodles, try these adorable Spaghetti and Meatballs Marinara! They look just like the classic recipe and feel the same, too.

PREP TIME: **15 minutes**
COOK TIME: **20 minutes**
SERVES: **4 people**

INGREDIENTS:

1 pound 85% lean ground beef

1 teaspoon dried oregano

1 teaspoon dried basil

Salt and pepper

1 tablespoon olive oil

2 cloves garlic, minced

2 cups marinara sauce

2 medium yellow squash

Chopped fresh basil, for garnish

INSTRUCTIONS:

1. Place the ground beef in a bowl, add the oregano and dried basil, and season with salt and pepper. Using your hands, combine the mixture well.

2. Shape the ground beef into ½-inch meatballs. You should be able to make about 30 small meatballs.

3. Heat the olive oil in a large pan over high heat and sear the meatballs for about 5 minutes total. Rotate them every now and then to ensure even cooking.

4. Reduce the heat to medium-low. Add the garlic and marinara sauce to the meatballs. Cover the pan and let it all simmer for about 15 minutes.

5. Trim the ends off the yellow squash and spiralize them into thick noodles.

6. When there is 3 minutes of cooking time left, add the noodles to the pan and mix them into the sauce well.

7. Garnish with the fresh basil and serve.

BEEFY ZOODLES MARINARA

One of our favorite, quick dinners is Beefy Zoodles Marinara. With only eight ingredients, it is a delicious, nutritious dinner that is ready in less than 30 minutes. You can also make this recipe with ground turkey or lamb.

PREP TIME: **5 minutes**
COOK TIME: **15 minutes**
SERVES: **4 people**

INGREDIENTS:

1 tablespoon olive oil

1 pound 90% lean ground beef

2 large zucchini

2 cups marinara sauce

1 Roma tomato, diced

1 teaspoon dried basil

1 teaspoon dried oregano

Salt and pepper

INSTRUCTIONS:

1. Heat the olive oil in a skillet over medium heat, add the ground beef and brown the meat until almost fully cooked, 7 to 8 minutes. Break it up well with a wooden spoon.

2. Meanwhile, trim the ends off the zucchini and spiralize them into thin noodles.

3. Remove the ground beef from the pan, place it in a bowl and lower the heat. Wipe up any excess oil from the skillet with a paper towel and add the zucchini noodles. Cook them over low heat for 2 minutes, tossing continuously.

4. Add the ground beef back to the pan along with marinara sauce and diced tomato. Season with the basil, oregano and salt and pepper, stir and let it simmer for 5 minutes to blend the flavors. Serve immediately.

APPLE AND GOAT CHEESE STUFFED PORK LOIN

Spiralizing isn't just for vegetables! Speed up your prep in the kitchen and add a fun texture to this Apple and Goat Cheese Stuffed Pork Loin by spiralizing an apple and cooking it down in a sage broth.

PREP TIME: 25 minutes
COOK TIME: 90 minutes
SERVES: 4 people

INGREDIENTS:

2 Granny Smith apples

2 tablespoons olive oil

1 white onion, diced

2 tablespoons unsalted butter

6 to 8 sage leaves

½ cup chicken broth

3 pounds pork loin

2 ounces goat cheese

Salt and pepper

INSTRUCTIONS:

1. Preheat the oven to 375°F.

2. Spiralize the apples into thin noodles and set aside.

3. Heat the olive oil in a large pan over medium heat, add the onion and cook until the onion is translucent, about 5 minutes.

4. Add the apple noodles and cook for 3 to 4 minutes.

5. Add the butter and sage leaves to the pan and decrease the heat to low. Simmer for about 2 minutes.

6. Add the chicken broth and let the mixture simmer until most of the chicken broth has evaporated, about 8-10 minutes.

7. Transfer the stuffing to a plate and let it cool.

8. Butterfly the pork loin and pound it gently.

9. Add the stuffing to the pork loin in a straight line along one side. Crumble the goat cheese along the stuffing.

10. Roll up the pork loin, pressing gently to distribute the stuffing.

11. Tie the pork loin with twine and season with salt and pepper.

12. Place in a baking dish and roast in the oven for about 90 minutes.

13. Remove the dish from the oven and allow it to rest for 10 minutes before cutting off the butcher's twine and slicing the pork widthwise.

PINEAPPLE JALAPEÑO PORK KEBABS WITH MARINATED SQUASH MEDLEY

Just because you're eating low carb doesn't mean you should cut out all fruit!
Some fun fruit every now and then is fine in moderation. A perfect example is our
Pineapple Jalapeño Pork Kebabs with Marinated Squash Medley.

PREP TIME: 2.5 hourss
COOK TIME: 15 minutes
SERVES: 4 people

INGREDIENTS:

Squash and Marinade

1 medium eggplant

Salt and pepper

2 tablespoons white vinegar

2 tablespoons lemon juice

2 cloves garlic, minced

⅓ cup olive oil

2 medium zucchini

2 medium yellow squash

Kebabs

1 pound pork tenderloin,
    cubed

2 tablespoons lemon juice

2 tablespoons soy sauce

Salt and pepper

8 ounces pineapple, cubed

2 fresh jalapeño peppers, cut
    into chunks

INSTRUCTIONS:

1. If you're using wooden skewers, first soak them in water.

2. To make the squash and marinade, cut the eggplant into 1-inch cubes. Salt the eggplant liberally and let it sit in a colander for 30 minutes. Rinse and pat dry.

3. Add the vinegar, lemon juice, garlic, and salt and pepper to taste to a medium mixing bowl and whisk to mix everything together. Gradually whisk in the oil until it is emulsified.

4. Trim and spiralize the zucchini and yellow squash.

5. Transfer the noodles and eggplant cubes to a large bowl and add half the marinade. Allow this to marinate for at least 2 hours.

6. To make the kebabs, add the pork cubes, lemon juice, soy sauce, and salt and pepper to taste to a mixing bowl and toss well.

7. Preheat the grill to medium-high heat (400°F to 450°F) and preheat the oven to 350°F.

8. Thread the pork, pineapple and jalapeño chunks alternately onto wooden skewers.

9. Grill each skewer for about 7 minutes on each side.

10. Transfer the eggplant and noodles to a baking dish and bake them for 10 to 15 minutes, tossing them gently if needed.

11. Place the skewers on a plate with the marinated noodles on the side. Drizzle the noodles with the remaining half of the marinade and serve.

BROWNED BUTTER PORK CHOPS WITH BUTTERNUT NOODLES

Browning your butter is a great way to add more flavor to dishes without a lot of added effort. Simply caramelize the butter a bit in a pan to release more of that buttery flavor! You'll be surprised what a difference it makes.

PREP TIME: 10 minutes
COOK TIME: 15 minutes
SERVES: 4 people

INGREDIENTS:

1 large butternut squash

Salt and pepper

8 tablespoons (½ cup or 1 stick) unsalted butter

2 tablespoons olive oil

4 (6-ounce) pork chops

Grated Parmesan cheese, for garnish

INSTRUCTIONS:

1. Preheat the oven to 450°F. Line a 13 x 9-inch baking sheet with parchment paper.

2. Cut off the ends of the squash. Peel the straighter half until you reach the bright orange inside. Spiralize the squash into thick noodles.

3. Put the butternut noodles into a large mixing bowl. Add salt and pepper to taste and mix well. Transfer to the prepared baking dish.

4. Melt the butter in a small pan over medium-high heat. After it fully melts, swirl the pan continuously to keep the butter moving while it browns. As soon as it turns light brown, remove it from the heat and pour it over the butternut noodles.

5. Transfer the baking dish to the oven and bake the noodles for 10 to 12 minutes. The edges of the noodles should be slightly browned.

6. In the meantime, heat the olive oil in a skillet over medium heat.

7. Season the pork chops with salt and pepper, add them to the skillet and fry them for 5 to 7 minutes on each side or until golden brown and firm to the touch.

8. Serve the pork chops with the noodles on the side topped with some grated Parmesan cheese.

PORK STIR-FRY

We love stir-fries! They're easy, quick and some of the most delicious dishes.
Give our veggie-filled Pork Stir-Fry a try and see how you like it!

PREP TIME: 10 minutes
COOK TIME: 20 minutes
SERVES: 4 people

INGREDIENTS:

24 ounces boneless pork loin

2 tablespoons olive oil

½ medium white onion, chopped

8 ounces white mushrooms, sliced

2 tablespoons soy sauce

4 cups broccoli florets

1 cup whole snap peas

2 cloves garlic, diced

Salt and pepper

2 large zucchini

1 tablespoon sesame oil

2 teaspoons toasted sesame seeds

INSTRUCTIONS:

1. Slice the pork into ½-inch-thick slices.

2. Heat the olive oil in a deep skillet or wok over medium heat, add the pork slices and cook them for about 5 minutes.

3. Trim the ends off the zucchini and spiralize them into thick noodles.

4. Add the chopped onion and mushrooms to the pan and cook for 5 to 7 minutes, until the onion becomes translucent.

5. Add the soy sauce, broccoli florets, snap peas, garlic, and salt and pepper to taste and continue to cook everything for another 5 minutes, stirring continuously.

6. Add the zucchini noodles to the pan along with the sesame oil. Let everything cook for 2 more minutes.

7. Garnish with the sesame seeds and serve.

HAM AND CHEDDAR JICAMA CASSEROLE

Casseroles are notoriously easy to make—simply dump and bake! Our Ham and Cheddar Jicama Casserole is the perfect example of how a short ingredients list and a quick prep time can equal a delicious meal.

PREP TIME: **15 minutes**
COOK TIME: **40 minutes**
SERVES: **6–8 people**

INGREDIENTS:

1 large jicama

2 large zucchini

2 teaspoons salt

1 teaspoon pepper

24 ounces ham steak

10 ounces sharp cheddar cheese

Chopped fresh parsley, for garnish

INSTRUCTIONS:

1. Preheat the oven to 350°F. Grease a 13 x 9-inch casserole dish.

2. Slice the jicama's end off and carefully cut the waxy skin off with a paring knife. Spiralize the jicama into thin noodles.

3. Trim the ends off the zucchini and spiralize them into thin noodles.

4. Combine the two noodles in a mixing bowl and season with salt and pepper.

5. Dice the ham steak into ½-inch cubes and shred the cheddar cheese.

6. Add the ham steak and cheddar cheese to the noodles and toss to combine.

7. Spread the mixture into the casserole dish in an even layer.

8. Bake the casserole for 40 minutes or until the top is slightly browned.

9. Garnish with the fresh parsley and cut into 6 to 8 servings.

SOY-GLAZED SALMON WITH BROCCOLI AND CARROT NOODLES

A quick marinade can be the difference between a dry, boring fish and a culinary masterpiece. Scallion and jalapeño soy sauce gives these salmon fillets salty and spicy notes that are perfect combined with hearty broccoli and carrot noodles.

PREP TIME: 30 minutes
COOK TIME: 10 minutes
SERVES: 4 people

INGREDIENTS:

1 fresh jalapeño, minced

1 bunch scallions, chopped

½ cup soy sauce

Juice of 1 lemon

4 (6-ounce) salmon fillets

4 broccoli stems

2 large carrots

2 tablespoons olive oil

Salt and pepper

INSTRUCTIONS:

1. Combine the jalapeño, scallions, soy sauce and lemon juice in a large bowl. Stir to combine and add the salmon fillets. Cover the bowl with plastic wrap and allow the salmon to marinate for at least 30 minutes in the refrigerator.

2. In the meantime, trim the ends off the broccoli stems and carrots and peel both veggies. Spiralize them both into thick noodles.

3. Heat 1 tablespoon of the olive oil in a skillet over medium heat, add the noodles and cook for about 5 minutes or until slightly softened. Season the noodles with salt and pepper to taste.

4. Heat the remaining 1 tablespoon of oil in another pan over medium heat, add the salmon fillets and cook for 5 to 7 minutes on each side. The salmon should flake easily with a fork.

5. Make a bed of broccoli and carrot noodles on each of 4 plates and place a salmon fillet on top, or shred the salmon and toss everything together.

CILANTRO LIME SALMON WITH BROCCOLI AND CARROT NOODLES

Citrus and seafood go hand in hand. Any time you've got a fresh baked salmon, the first thing you should do is squeeze some lemon or lime on it. Or you can try this Cilantro Lime Salmon recipe and bake the salmon with citrus to bake the flavors right in!

PREP TIME: 10 minutes
COOK TIME: 15 minutes
SERVES: 4 people

INGREDIENTS:

1 cup chopped fresh cilantro

2 cloves garlic

Juice of 1 lime

3 tablespoons olive oil

4 (6-ounce) salmon fillets

Salt and pepper

4 broccoli stems

2 medium carrots

INSTRUCTIONS:

1. Preheat the oven to 400°F. Line a 13 x 9-inch baking sheet with foil.

2. Using a food processor or blender, puree the cilantro, garlic, lime juice and 1 tablespoon of the olive oil together.

3. Spread 1 tablespoon of olive oil evenly on the prepared baking sheet and place the salmon fillets, skin side down, on top.

4. Season the salmon with salt and pepper and spread the cilantro lime sauce over the top. Bake for 10 to 15 minutes or until the fish is easily flaked with a fork.

5. In the meantime, peel the broccoli stems and carrots and spiralize them into thick noodles.

6. Heat the remaining 1 tablespoon of oil in a large pan over medium heat, add the noodles and cook for 3 to 5 minutes, tossing continuously, until they've slightly softened. Season with salt and pepper to taste.

7. Serve the salmon on a bed of broccoli and carrot noodles with any of the remaining cilantro lime sauce from the pan.

SPICY NOODLE TUNA TARTARE BOWL

Tuna tartare may sound fancy, but it's nothing more than sushi-grade raw fish and lots of flavor!
In fact, it's a no-bake, no-fuss recipe that is ready before you even know it.
Enjoy the authentic Asian taste without the take-out.

PREP TIME: 15 minutes
COOK TIME: 0 minutes
SERVES: 4 people

INGREDIENTS:

24 ounces sushi-grade tuna

1 large avocado, pitted and
    peeled

¼ cup mayonnaise

2 tablespoons soy sauce

1 teaspoon Dijon mustard

2 teaspoons sriracha sauce
    (optional)

1 cucumber

Salt and pepper

Sesame seeds, for garnish

INSTRUCTIONS:

1. Dice the fresh tuna and avocado into small cubes and add
   them to a mixing bowl.

2. Combine the mayonnaise, soy sauce, mustard and sriracha,
   if using, in a small bowl, pour over the tuna and avocado and
   mix them gently.

3. Trim the ends off the cucumber and peel it. Spiralize it into
   thick noodles and add it to the mixing bowl. Season with
   salt and pepper to taste and toss all the ingredients well.

4. Garnish each serving with sesame seeds.

PARMESAN-CRUSTED COD WITH BROCCOLI NOODLES

You don't need bread to have the perfect breading! Parmesan cheese alone will do the trick just fine. We like to bake our cod in a Parmesan crust to both season the fish and add a fun crunch.

PREP TIME: 15 minutes
COOK TIME: 15 minutes
SERVES: 4 people

INGREDIENTS:

1 large egg

⅓ cup grated Parmesan cheese

1 teaspoon garlic powder

Salt and pepper

4 (6-ounce) cod fillets

4 broccoli stems

2 tablespoons olive oil

Shaved Parmesan, for garnish

INSTRUCTIONS:

1. Preheat the oven to 450°F. Line a 13 x 9-inch baking sheet with foil and grease the foil.

2. Beat the egg in a wide bowl.

3. In another bowl, mix the Parmesan cheese with the garlic powder and salt and pepper to taste and spread the mixture out evenly on a large, shallow plate.

4. Dredge the cod fillets evenly in the egg and then gently press each one in the Parmesan cheese mixture until they're all fully coated.

5. Arrange the fillets carefully in the prepared baking dish, making sure each has room and they aren't touching.

6. Bake the fillets for 10 to 15 minutes, or until they turn golden brown.

7. Meanwhile, trim the ends of the broccoli stems and peel them. Spiralize them into thick noodles.

8. Heat the oil in a skillet over medium heat, add the broccoli noodles and cook for 2 to 3 minutes, tossing continuously until they've slightly softened.

9. Make a bed of the cooked broccoli noodles on each of 4 plates, place a cod fillet on top and garnish with the shaved Parmesan cheese to serve.

SPICY SHRIMP AND MUSHROOM ZOODLES

Our Spicy Shrimp and Mushroom Zoodles is another dish that looks impressive but uses only common ingredients. This recipe has both Italian and Asian influences—our two favorite cuisines!

PREP TIME: **15 minutes**
COOK TIME: **15 minutes**
SERVES: **4 people**

INGREDIENTS:

1 tablespoon olive oil

8 ounces baby bella or white mushrooms, sliced

2 cloves garlic, minced

1 pound large shrimp, peeled and deveined

½ teaspoon dried basil

½ teaspoon red pepper flakes

Salt and pepper

2 zucchini

1 cup marinara sauce

2 tablespoons grated Parmesan cheese

Chopped fresh basil, for garnish

INSTRUCTIONS:

1. Heat the olive oil in a large pan over high heat. Add the sliced mushrooms and let them cook until slightly browned, about 5-7 minutes.

2. Add the minced garlic to the pan and cook for about 5 minutes longer, or until the garlic is fragrant.

3. Next, add the shrimp and cook for 2 to 3 minutes on each side, or until pink throughout. Season it all with the dried basil, red pepper flakes and salt and pepper to taste.

4. Remove the mixture from the pan, place in a bowl and let it rest while you prepare the noodles.

5. Trim the ends off the zucchini and spiralize them into thin noodles.

6. Lower the heat, add the marinara sauce to the same pan and allow it to come to a simmer. Add the zoodles and let them cook for about 5 minutes, or until softened, tossing continuously.

7. Add the shrimp mixture back into the pan and toss well to combine.

8. Serve with a sprinkle of grated Parmesan cheese and fresh basil to garnish.

RAINBOW SHRIMP STIR-FRY

When food looks good, you can't help but try it! That's why Rainbow Shrimp Stir-Fry is great to bring to parties or serve for dinner. The gorgeous colors come from every ingredient in the recipe. It's doesn't hurt that this stir-fry tastes amazing either!

PREP TIME: 8 minutes
COOK TIME: 15 minutes
SERVES: 4 people

INGREDIENTS:

2 tablespoons olive oil

½ large red onion

2 yellow bell peppers

2 medium zucchini

2 medium carrots

Salt and pepper

24 ounces large shrimp, peeled and deveined

1 cup shelled edamame

4 fresh basil leaves, chopped

INSTRUCTIONS:

1. Heat the olive oil in a skillet over medium heat. Chop the onion and peppers into thin strips, add them to the pan and cook them until softened, about 5 minutes.

2. Trim the ends off the zucchini and carrots and peel the carrots. Spiralize both vegetables into thin noodles and add them to the pan. Season with salt and pepper to taste and let them cook for 3 minutes, or until softened a bit.

3. Remove the veggies from the pan, place in a bowl and add the shrimp and edamame to the pan. Cook for 3 to 5 minutes, flipping the shrimp, until all the shrimp turn pink.

4. Return the cooked noodles to the pan and toss to combine.

5. Divide equally and garnish with the chopped basil leaves.

LEMON GINGER SCALLOPS ON ROASTED BUTTERNUT RIBBONS

We dressed these delicate scallops with a citrusy sauce to brighten up the deep, roasted flavor of the butternut squash ribbons. The combo makes a great dinner in every season!

PREP TIME: 10 minutes
COOK TIME: 20 minutes
SERVES: 4 people

INGREDIENTS:

Noodles

2 butternut squash

2 tablespoons coconut oil, melted

1 teaspoon salt

Scallops

2 tablespoons olive oil

Juice of 1 lemon

1-inch cube ginger, grated

Salt and pepper

16 scallops

Lemon zest, for garnish

INSTRUCTIONS:

1. Preheat the oven to 400°F. Line a 13 x 9-inch baking sheet with foil.

2. To make the noodles, cut off the bulbous half of each butternut squash. Cut the end of the straighter half off and peel its hard skin multiple times until you reach the bright orange inside. Spiralize the butternut squash into ribbons.

3. In a large mixing bowl, toss the butternut squash ribbons in the melted coconut oil and salt and then arrange them evenly on the prepared baking sheet.

4. Bake the butternut squash ribbons for 10 minutes. Turn on the broiler and broil the ribbons for 2 to 3 minutes, or until they've browned slightly.

5. Meanwhile, to make the scallops, in a large bowl, whisk together the olive oil, lemon juice, grated ginger and salt and pepper to taste.

6. Add the scallops to the bowl and toss gently to combine. Let this sit for about 10 minutes.

7. Heat a frying pan over high heat until hot, add the scallops with a bit of their marinade and cook for 4 minutes on each side, or until they are lightly browned on each side.

8. Divide the roasted butternut squash ribbons among 4 plates, top each pile with 4 scallops, sprinkle with lemon zest and serve.

SHRIMP SQUASH ALFREDO

Creamy, cheesy and hearty, Shrimp Squash Alfredo is surprisingly easy to make.
It can be ready in less than 30 minutes, so it's perfect for any busy weekday
when you still want to dine like a king or queen.

PREP TIME: 15 minutes
COOK TIME: 10 minutes
SERVES: 4 people

INGREDIENTS:

Alfredo Sauce

1 tablespoon olive oil

1 clove garlic, crushed

4 tablespoons butter

1 cup heavy cream

¼ cup grated Parmesan
    cheese, plus more
    for garnish

1 teaspoon dried parsley

Salt and pepper

Shrimp and Noodles

1 tablespoon olive oil

1 pound large shrimp, peeled
    and deveined

2 large yellow squash

Salt and pepper

Chopped fresh basil,
    for garnish

INSTRUCTIONS:

1. To make the sauce, heat the olive oil in a small skillet over low heat, add the garlic and cook until it is fragrant, about 1 minute.

2. Add the butter and cook for about 2 minutes, until melted, then add the heavy cream. Stir well to combine.

3. Add 1 tablespoon of the grated Parmesan cheese at a time, stirring until each is melted before adding the next.

4. Season the sauce with the dried parsley and salt and pepper to taste. Remove the pan from the heat and set the sauce aside to thicken a bit while you prepare the shrimp and noodles.

5. To make the shrimp and noodles, heat the olive oil in a large skillet over medium heat, add the large shrimp and cook for about 3 minutes on each side, or until pink throughout.

6. Trim the ends off the yellow squash and spiralize them into thick noodles. Add them to the pan with the shrimp and toss very well. Season it all with more salt and pepper.

7. Add the Alfredo sauce, stir to combine and cook for 3 to 4 minutes, or until the noodles have softened up a bit.

8. Garnish the Shrimp Squash Alfredo with a sprinkle of Parmesan cheese and fresh basil and serve.

AVOCADO LIME SCALLOPS AND YELLOW SQUASH SPAGHETTI

Avocado is extremely versatile! One of our favorite ways to use up avocados before they go bad is to make sauces with them. Avocado's creamy and mild flavor goes great with just about anything—like Avocado Lime Scallops and Yellow Squash Spaghetti!

PREP TIME: 20 minutes
COOK TIME: 20 minutes
SERVES: 4 people

INGREDIENTS:

2 tablespoons olive oil

12 scallops

Noodles

1 tablespoon unsalted butter

2 cloves garlic

2 yellow squash

Avocado Lime Sauce

1 medium avocado

Juice of 1 lime

2 tablespoons avocado oil or olive oil

2 tablespoons mayonnaise

Salt and pepper

INSTRUCTIONS:

1. Heat the oil in a large skillet over high heat, add the scallops and cook for 4 minutes on each side, or until lightly browned on each side.

2. To make the noodles, melt the butter in another large pan over medium heat and use a garlic press to squeeze the garlic cloves directly into the pan. Let this cook until fragrant, but not brown.

3. Trim the ends off the yellow squash and spiralize them into thick noodles. Add them to the pan with the garlic and let them cook for about 3 minutes, tossing continuously. Remove the pan from the heat while you prepare the sauce.

4. To make the sauce, cut open the avocado, remove the pit and scoop the flesh into the bowl of a food processor. Add the lime juice, avocado oil, mayonnaise, and salt and pepper to taste to the food processor and blend everything until it reaches a smooth consistency.

5. Make a bed of noodles on each of 4 plates, add a good dollop of the Avocado Lime Sauce and place 3 scallops on top. Serve.

SPINACH AND CRÈME FRAÎCHE FRITTATA

Spinach and Crème Fraîche Frittata is fit for breakfast, lunch or dinner! It's hearty and creamy and has a great texture thanks to the fun zucchini and parsnip noodles. If you don't have crème fraîche, feel free to use sour cream!

PREP TIME: 20 minutes
COOK TIME: 15 minutes
SERVES: 8 people

INGREDIENTS:

2 tablespoons olive oil

1 white onion, diced

24 ounces fresh spinach

2 zucchini

1 medium parsnip

Salt and pepper

8 large eggs

6 ounces crème fraîche or
  sour cream

½ cup shredded mozzarella
  cheese

INSTRUCTIONS:

1. Preheat the oven to 350°F.

2. Heat the olive oil in a large oven-safe skillet over medium heat, add the white onion and cook until the onion is translucent, about 5 minutes.

3. Add the fresh spinach to the pan a few handfuls at a time until all of it has wilted.

4. Trim the ends off the zucchini and parsnip and peel the parsnip. Spiralize them both into thin noodles.

5. Add the noodles to the pan and let them cook for about 5 minutes, tossing continuously. Season them with salt and pepper.

6. Meanwhile, crack the eggs into a mixing bowl and whisk very well. Add the crème fraîche and whisk vigorously to disperse it a bit.

7. Add the whisked eggs to the pan, covering all the spinach and pressing the noodles in so they're completely submerged.

8. Transfer the pan to the hot oven and bake for about 10 minutes, or until the eggs are set.

9. Take the frittata out and add the shredded mozzarella cheese over the whole top. Turn on the broiler and broil the frittata for about 2 minutes, keeping an eye on the cheese so it doesn't burn.

10. Cut the frittata into slices and serve.

BACON CHEDDAR ZUCCHINI FRITTERS

Fritters are a fun dinner for kids and adults alike. These savory Bacon Cheddar Zucchini Fritters are full of crunchy bacon bits and creamy cheddar cheese. The outsides are perfectly crispy with soft centers. Best of all, these fritters are low carb and gluten-free!

PREP TIME: 15 minutes
COOK TIME: 30 minutes
SERVES: 4 people

INGREDIENTS:

2 to 3 cups avocado oil

2 zucchini

2 tablespoons salt

12 bacon strips, cooked and crumbled

6 ounces shredded cheddar cheese

2 cloves garlic

2 large eggs

3 tablespoons coconut flour

Salt and pepper

Sour cream, for garnish

Chopped chives, for garnish

INSTRUCTIONS:

1. Heat the avocado oil in a small pot over high heat while you prepare the recipe. If you don't have avocado oil, use any other mild-tasting oil with a high smoke point, like coconut oil.

2. Trim the ends off the zucchini and spiralize them into thin noodles. Add them to a strainer set over a large bowl and sprinkle them generously with salt. Let the noodles sit for about 30 minutes so that some of the water can drain from them. Squeeze the noodles gently with a paper towel to get some excess water out. Discard the excess water.

3. Combine the drained noodles with the crumbled bacon and shredded cheddar in a mixing bowl.

4. Use a garlic press to squeeze the garlic cloves into the bowl and add the eggs and coconut flour. Season with salt and pepper and mix everything very well with your hands.

5. Grab handfuls of the mixture and start shaping them into thin patties 4 to 5 inches in diameter.

6. Test if the oil is ready by either using a thermometer (it should read 350°F) or by dipping a strand of zucchini in. If the oil takes more than 2 seconds to start sizzling, it's not ready.

7. When the oil is at the right temperature, gently lower 1 or 2 fritters in at a time and fry them for about 6 minutes. Flip them a few times to ensure one side doesn't get too brown.

8. Serve warm with a dollop of sour cream and chopped chives.

BACON AND BROCCOLI CARBONARA

This twist on the classic carbonara makes it lighter yet full of flavor. Yellow squash complements the savory flavors of Bacon and Broccoli Carbonara and makes you want seconds!

PREP TIME: **15 minutes**
COOK TIME: **10 minutes**
SERVES: **4–6 people**

INGREDIENTS:

12 strips bacon

4 ounces broccoli florets

3 yellow squash

3 large eggs

¼ cup grated Parmesan cheese

¼ cup heavy cream

½ tablespoon garlic powder

Salt and pepper

Chopped fresh basil, for garnish

INSTRUCTIONS:

1. Add the bacon strips to a cold pan, turn on the heat to medium and allow them to cook, flipping once, until they're an even brown and slightly crispy. This should take 5-10 minutes, depending on the thickness of the bacon.

2. When some of the fat has rendered off the bacon, add the broccoli florets and fry them in the bacon fat until the bacon is crispy and the broccoli is bright green and slightly softened. Transfer the broccoli and bacon to a paper towel–lined plate to drain.

3. Trim the ends off the yellow squash and spiralize the squash into thin noodles.

4. Whisk together the eggs, Parmesan cheese, heavy cream and garlic powder in a bowl.

5. Wipe out any excess bacon fat and add the noodles to the pan over low heat. Add the egg mixture right away and let everything cook, stirring, until the Parmesan is melted and the noodles are soft, about 5 minutes.

6. Chop the bacon strips into small bits once they have cooled off a bit.

7. Add the chopped bacon and broccoli florets to the pan. Season with salt and pepper and toss to combine everything.

8. Divide evenly among 4 to 6 plates and garnish with the fresh chopped basil.

LASAGNA ROSETTES

We love lasagna. It can be a chore to make, especially when it's low-carb.
We put a new spin on lasagna by deconstructing it and creating single-size
portions that are easy to assemble and super fun to eat!

PREP TIME: **15** minutes
COOK TIME: **15** minutes
SERVES: **4** people (2 rosettes per serving)

INGREDIENTS:

2 large zucchini

1 cup whole-milk ricotta

6 large eggs

½ teaspoon salt

¼ teaspoon pepper

½ teaspoon dried basil

½ teaspoon dried oregano

½ cup shredded mozzarella
cheese

8 tablespoons tomato paste

Shaved or grated Parmesan
cheese, for garnish

INSTRUCTIONS:

1. Preheat the oven to 350°F. Grease 8 cups of a 12-cup
   muffin tin.

2. Trim the ends off the zucchini and spiralize them into ribbons.

3. Add a handful of ribbons to each of the prepared muffin
   cups, reserving some for the top.

4. Scoop the ricotta cheese into the center of a clean kitchen
   towel or piece of cheesecloth folded a few times, draw the
   corners of the cloth together, twist the cloth and squeeze
   some of the excess moisture out of the ricotta cheese. This
   will make the end result set much better. We recommend
   not skipping this step.

5. In a mixing bowl, whisk together the eggs, drained ricotta,
   salt, pepper, basil and oregano. Pour the mixture over the
   zucchini ribbons, making sure to get it into all the crevices.

6. Add a bit of the shredded mozzarella cheese to each rosette
   as well as 1 tablespoon of tomato paste in the center.

7. Add some of the reserved bits of zucchini ribbons to the tops
   to garnish and make each one look like petals of a flower.

8. Transfer the muffin pan to the oven and bake for 15
   minutes. The rosettes should be set on top. Remove the pan
   from the oven and then let the rosettes cool on a wire rack
   for about 20 minutes to help them set. Remove the rosettes
   from the muffin cups.

9. Serve warm with a sprinkle of Parmesan cheese.

LASAGNAROLE

Who doesn't love a good casserole? We added fun zucchini noodles to the classic flavors of lasagna to create a fusion of two family-favorite dinners. Our Lasagnarole is easy to make and super fun for kids!

PREP TIME: 15 minutes
COOK TIME: 35 minutes
SERVES: 6 people

INGREDIENTS:

3 large zucchini

Salt and pepper

1 tablespoon olive oil

1 pound 85% lean ground beef

1 teaspoon dried basil

1 teaspoon dried oregano

1 teaspoon garlic powder

2 cups ricotta cheese

1 cup marinara sauce

1 cup shredded mozzarella cheese

¼ cup shaved or grated Parmesan cheese, plus more for garnish

Chopped fresh basil leaves, for garnish

INSTRUCTIONS:

1. Preheat the oven to 350°F. Grease a 9 x 13-inch baking dish.

2. Trim and spiralize the zucchini. In a colander, salt the noodles generously with salt. Let the noodles sit for 30 minutes to drain water. Squeeze the noodles gently with a paper towel to get some excess water out as well. Discard the excess water.

3. In a pan with the olive oil over high heat, brown the ground beef, breaking it up into smaller pieces with a wooden spoon.

4. Season the beef with the basil, oregano, garlic powder and salt and pepper to taste. Stir well to combine the seasonings and meat and then remove the pan from the heat while you prepare the noodles.

5. Transfer the drained noodles to a mixing bowl and add the ricotta cheese, marinara sauce, ½ cup of the shredded mozzarella and the shaved Parmesan cheese.

6. Mix in the ground beef. Transfer the mixture to the baking dish and bake for 30 minutes.

7. After 30 minutes, sprinkle the remaining ½ cup of mozzarella cheese evenly across the top of the Lasagnarole.

8. Turn on the broiler and broil the casserole for 3 to 5 minutes, keeping a close eye on the cheese, until the top is evenly browned. Remove the Lasagnarole from the oven and let it cool for 10 to 15 minutes to help it set.

9. Serve with some shaved Parmesan and fresh basil leaves.

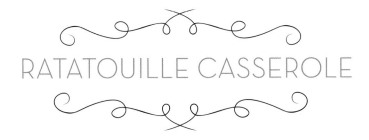

RATATOUILLE CASSEROLE

Ratatouille is great in the summer or winter; you really can't go wrong! It's a breeze to make and kids love all the colors and layers in the dish. Try out this Ratatouille Casserole with your kids and have fun arranging everything beautifully!

PREP TIME: 25 minutes
COOK TIME: 45 minutes
SERVES: 4–6 people

INGREDIENTS:

1 cup marinara sauce

1 small yellow onion

1 medium yellow squash

1 medium zucchini

3 Campari tomatoes

1 small eggplant

½ teaspoon dried basil

½ teaspoon dried oregano

Salt and pepper

4 ounces shredded
    mozzarella cheese

Chopped fresh basil,
    for garnish

INSTRUCTIONS:

1. Preheat the oven to 400°F.

2. Spread half of the marinara sauce in the bottom of a 13 x 9-inch casserole dish or any deep oven-safe dish.

3. Spiralize the onion into thin strips by using the ribbon attachment on your spiralizer and lay the slices evenly over the marinara sauce.

4. Trim the ends off the yellow squash and zucchini and spiralize them into ribbons. Spread the ribbons evenly across the entire dish.

5. Slice the tomatoes and eggplant into 1-inch cubes and fit them in within the ribbons.

6. Season the dish with the dried basil, oregano and salt and pepper to taste. Add the remaining half of the marinara sauce on top of the vegetables.

7. Cover the dish with foil and bake the casserole for 30 minutes.

8. Remove the foil after 30 minutes and sprinkle the shredded mozzarella on top. Return the casserole to the oven and bake for another 10 to 15 minutes, or until the cheese is lightly browned.

9. Allow the casserole to rest for 5 minutes after removing it from the oven. Garnish with the chopped fresh basil and serve.

SIDES

GREEK ZOODLE SALAD

The Greek Zoodle Salad is a go-to salad in our home for dinner with grilled chicken breasts or sausages. It's quick and easy to make and calls for common ingredients. If needed, you can skip the olives or feta and still end up with a delicious traditional garden salad.

PREP TIME: 10 minutes
COOK TIME: 0 minutes
SERVES: 4 people

INGREDIENTS:

2 medium cucumbers

20 cherry tomatoes

20 Kalamata olives, pitted

½ red onion, diced

2 tablespoons olive oil

1 teaspoon white vinegar

2 teaspoons dried oregano

Salt and pepper

2 ounces feta cheese

INSTRUCTIONS:

1. Trim the ends off the cucumbers and spiralize them into thick noodles. Add the noodles to a large mixing bowl.

2. Cut the cherry tomatoes and olives in half and add them and the diced onion to the bowl.

3. Add the olive oil, vinegar, oregano, and salt and pepper to taste and mix everything well.

4. Crumble the feta cheese on top and serve.

CACIO E PEPE

Cacio e pepe is a classic Italian staple for any dinner. The name translates into "cheese and pepper" and this recipe is full of just that—Parmesan cheese and freshly cracked black pepper to make the perfect combo!

PREP TIME: 5 minutes
COOK TIME: 10 minutes
SERVES: 4 people

INGREDIENTS:

2 tablespoons olive oil

1 teaspoon cracked black pepper, plus more for garnish

2 tablespoons unsalted butter

4 yellow squash

4 tablespoons grated Parmigiano-Reggiano cheese

1 handful shaved Parmesan cheese, for garnish

INSTRUCTIONS:

1. Heat the olive oil in a pan over medium heat.

2. Add the cracked black pepper and let it warm up in the olive oil until fragrant and almost sizzling, about 2 minutes.

3. Lower the heat, add the butter and let it melt gently.

4. Trim the ends off the yellow squash and spiralize them into thick noodles. Add them to the melted butter and oil in the pan. Toss quickly with tongs to combine and coat them evenly.

5. Right away, add 1 tablespoon of the grated Parmigiano-Reggiano cheese, tossing to help it melt. Once it has melted, add the remaining 3 tablespoons of Parmigiano-Reggiano, 1 tablespoon at a time, stirring to coat the noodles.

6. Divide among 4 plates, sprinkle with more black pepper and the shaved Parmesan cheese to garnish and serve.

MAPLE PECAN BUTTERNUT SQUASH NOODLES

Not all vegetables have to be savory! This sweet side dish of Maple Pecan Butternut Squash Noodles is perfect for hearty meats like turkey or pork. Enjoy this recipe during Thanksgiving or anytime you're looking for an interesting twist!

PREP TIME: **10 minutes**
COOK TIME: **10 minutes**
SERVES: 4–6 people

INGREDIENTS:

2 large butternut squash

2 tablespoons unsalted butter

2 ounces pecans, whole or crushed

¼ cup 100% pure maple syrup

¼ teaspoon salt

¼ teaspoon ground cinnamon, plus more for garnish

INSTRUCTIONS:

1. Cut off the ends of the squash. Peel the straighter half until you reach the bright orange inside. Spiralize the squash into thick noodles.

2. In a large pan over medium heat, melt the butter until slightly browned, and then add the pecans. Let them toast for 3 to 5 minutes to deepen their flavor.

3. Add the butternut squash noodles and let them cook, stirring occasionally, for about 8 minutes, or until they've softened a bit and absorbed some butter.

4. Add the maple syrup, salt and cinnamon. Stir the noodles.

5. Garnish with an extra sprinkle of cinnamon and serve.

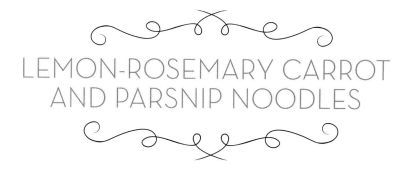

LEMON-ROSEMARY CARROT AND PARSNIP NOODLES

From the satisfying crunch to the sweet and savory flavors of the dressing, this Lemon-Rosemary Carrot and Parsnip side will have you falling in love at first bite.

PREP TIME: 10 minutes
COOK TIME: 0 minutes
SERVES: 4 people

INGREDIENTS:

2 large carrots

2 large parsnips

Chopped fresh parsley,
for garnish

Dressing

1 teaspoon honey

Juice of ½ lemon

1 teaspoon Dijon mustard

½ teaspoon dried rosemary

¼ cup olive oil

Salt and pepper

INSTRUCTIONS:

1. Trim the ends off the carrots and parsnips, peel them both and spiralize them into thin noodles.

2. To make the dressing, in a small bowl whisk the honey, lemon juice, mustard and rosemary together. Slowly add the olive oil, 1 tablespoon at a time, whisking until you've added all of the oil. Add salt and pepper to taste.

3. Toss the noodles with the dressing, garnish with the fresh parsley and serve.

GARLIC AND HERB BUTTERNUT SQUASH FRITTERS

Our low-carb and gluten-free Garlic and Herb Butternut Squash Fritters have hints of both sweet and savory! They're perfect for an unexpected dinner side, plus they're fun to make. We recommend preparing the herb butter the day before making the fritters.

PREP TIME: 15 minutes
COOK TIME: 30 minutes
SERVES: 4 people

INGREDIENTS:

Herb Butter

5 or 6 fresh basil leaves

2 fresh mint leaves

1 bunch fresh tarragon

1 bunch fresh parsley

8 tablespoons (½ cup or 1 stick) unsalted butter, at room temperature

½ teaspoon salt

Fritters

2 to 3 cups avocado oil

2 butternut squash

2 cloves garlic

1 large egg

2 tablespoons coconut flour

Salt and pepper

INSTRUCTIONS:

1. To make the herb butter, mince all the herbs very finely and add them to a small bowl. Add the softened butter and salt, and stir to thoroughly combine the ingredients.

2. Add the butter mixture to a sheet of plastic wrap and roll it tightly into a log shape. Refrigerate it overnight so it will be ready for the fritters the next day.

3. To make the fritters, heat the avocado oil (or any mild-tasting oil with a high smoke point, like coconut oil) in a small pot over high heat while you prepare the batter.

4. Cut off the bulbous half of the butternut squash. Cut the end of the straighter half off and peel its hard skin multiple times until you reach the bright orange inside. Spiralize the butternut squash into thin noodles and place them in a deep mixing bowl.

5. Run some kitchen shears through the noodles a few times to cut them into shorter strands. This will help the patties stay a uniform size.

6. Use a garlic press to squeeze the garlic cloves into the butternut squash noodles.

7. Add the egg and coconut flour. If you don't have coconut flour, use your favorite gluten-free flour, though you may need to use a bit more of it.

8. Season with salt and pepper and use your hands to coat the noodles and mix everything together until all the noodles are covered in a batterlike coating.

9. Take handfuls of noodles and squeeze them into flat patties 4 to 5 inches in diameter. You should get 8 patties.

10. Test the oil by dipping a strand of noodle into it. If it takes more than 1 to 2 seconds to sizzle, the oil is not hot enough. Or use a thermometer to test the heat; it should be 375°F.

11. Lower in one fritter at a time and let it fry for about 6 minutes. Toward the end, flip it over a few times to prevent one side from frying and browning too much.

12. Transfer the fritter to a paper towel–lined plate to drain and repeat the process with the rest of the fritters.

13. Add 1 tablespoon of the herb butter to each fritter and serve.

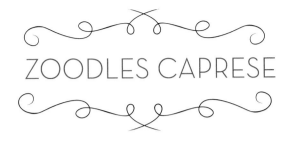

ZOODLES CAPRESE

Zoodles Caprese is a favorite for barbecues, potlucks, and family gatherings because the ingredients list is short and sweet. This recipe is bursting with fresh flavors and requires no cook time!

PREP TIME: **10 minutes**
COOK TIME: **0 minutes**
SERVES: **4–6 people**

INGREDIENTS:

3 large zucchini

8 ounces cherry tomatoes

4 ounces fresh mozzarella balls

2 tablespoons olive oil

2 tablespoons balsamic vinegar

Salt and pepper

6 to 10 large fresh basil leaves

INSTRUCTIONS:

1. Trim the ends off the zucchini and spiralize them into thin noodles. Add them to a deep mixing bowl.

2. Add the cherry tomatoes and fresh mozzarella balls.

3. Dress the zoodles with the olive oil, balsamic vinegar, and salt and pepper to taste.

4. Roughly chop the fresh basil leaves, add to the bowl and toss the zoodles to coat everything evenly. Serve immediately.

CREAMY APPLE SLAW

You'll find hidden sugar lurking everywhere . . . but not in this Creamy Apple Slaw!
We used the natural sweetness from a crisp apple to sweeten our coleslaw
and added extra tartness using apple cider vinegar.

PREP TIME: 15 minutes
COOK TIME: 0 minutes
SERVES: 4 people

INGREDIENTS:

1 head of green cabbage

1 large carrot

1 Gala apple (or your favorite apple)

2 scallions, chopped

2 ounces pecans, whole or chopped

1 teaspoon poppy seeds

¼ cup mayonnaise

½ cup sour cream

1 tablespoon apple cider vinegar

Salt and pepper

INSTRUCTIONS:

1. Using the ribbon attachment on your spiralizer, shred the head of cabbage into a deep mixing bowl.

2. Trim the ends off the carrot, peel it and spiralize it into thin noodles. Cut the noodles with kitchen shears to make shorter segments. Add them to the shredded cabbage.

3. Using a cheese grater on its medium side, shred the apple into the mixing bowl.

4. Add the chopped scallion, pecans and poppy seeds to the bowl.

5. Combine the mayonnaise, sour cream, apple cider vinegar, and salt and pepper to taste in a small bowl. Pour over the slaw and toss everything very well to combine.

6. Chill the Creamy Apple Slaw in the refrigerator before serving. Serve chilled.

JICAMA HASH BROWNS

Jicama is a great substitute for potatoes in many different recipes. One of the easiest is Jicama Hash Browns. Breakfast for dinner is always the best!

PREP TIME: 10 minutes
COOK TIME: 30 minutes
SERVES: 4 people

INGREDIENTS:

1 large jicama

1 large egg, beaten

2 tablespoons coconut flour

1 teaspoon paprika

Pinch of cayenne (optional)

Salt and pepper

2 tablespoons unsalted butter, plus more for serving

INSTRUCTIONS:

1. Slice the ends off the jicama and carefully cut the waxy skin off with a paring knife. Spiralize the jicama into thin noodles.

2. In a medium bowl, combine the noodles with the egg and coconut flour and use your hands to mix and coat everything evenly.

3. Season the mixture with the paprika, cayenne (if using) and salt and pepper to taste.

4. Mix everything once again and, using your hands, start forming flat, round patties about 2 inches in diameter.

5. Heat the butter in a frying pan over medium heat until slightly browned, then fry each hash brown for about 5 minutes on each side. The outsides of the hash browns should be browned and crispy, while the insides should remain soft.

6. Serve the Jicama Hash Browns hot with an extra smear of butter.

PESTO TOMATO ZOODLES

A good pesto recipe is great to have on hand to add intense flavor to any meal. We love the combination of bold pesto and the sweet pops of cherry tomatoes in Pesto Tomato Zoodles. They can be enjoyed raw or cooked!

PREP TIME: 10 minutes
COOK TIME: 0–5 minutes
SERVES: 4–6 people

INGREDIENTS:

Pesto

1 cup fresh basil leaves, plus more for garnish

2 tablespoons pine nuts

2 tablespoons grated Parmesan cheese

1 clove garlic

Salt and pepper

¼ cup olive oil

Noodles

3 medium zucchini

1 cup cherry tomatoes

INSTRUCTIONS:

1. To make the pesto, combine the basil, pine nuts, Parmesan, garlic and salt and pepper to taste in a food processor and blend them until they are smooth.

2. While blending, slowly pour in the olive oil to create an emulsion. If you can't pour while blending, just pour in about 1 tablespoon of oil at a time and blend after each addition.

3. To make the noodles, trim the ends off the zucchini and spiralize them into thin or thick noodles according to your preference.

4. Optional: If you prefer cooked zucchini, lightly fry the zucchini in a lightly oiled pan over medium heat for 3 to 5 minutes, tossing continuously.

5. Combine the zucchini noodles and pesto in a mixing bowl. Add the cherry tomatoes and mix with a wooden spoon until everything is evenly coated.

6. Divide into even portions and garnish with fresh basil leaves.

JICAMA SHOESTRING FRIES
WITH ROMESCO DIP

Just one jicama can make so many fun shoestring fries! They're a great substitute for popcorn or regular curly fries and can be snacked on and dipped for hours.

PREP TIME: **10 minutes**
COOK TIME: **15 minutes**
SERVES: **4 people**

INGREDIENTS:

2 to 3 cups avocado oil

2 large jicamas

Salt and pepper

Romesco Dip

1 large tomato

½ cup raw almonds

3 tablespoons olive oil

Salt and pepper

1 teaspoon white vinegar

2 cloves garlic

INSTRUCTIONS:

1. Heat the avocado oil (or any mild-tasting oil with a high smoke point, like coconut oil) in a small pot over high heat, making sure there is about 1 inch of oil.

2. Slice the ends off the jicamas and carefully cut the waxy skin off with a paring knife.

3. Spiralize the jicamas into thin noodles.

4. Test the oil by dipping a strand of jicama into it. If it takes more than 1 to 2 seconds to sizzle, the oil is not hot enough. Or use a thermometer to test the heat; it should be 375°F.

5. Add a handful of the spiralized jicama to the oil and deep-fry it until it turns a light brown color. Remove the jicama with a slotted spoon and place it on a paper towel–lined plate to absorb the excess oil and cool down. Repeat this step until you've fried all of the jicama.

6. Season each batch of Jicama Shoestring Fries with salt and pepper while they're still hot.

7. To make the Romesco dip, blend all the dip ingredients together in a food processor until they reach a smooth consistency.

8. Serve the Jicama Shoestring Fries with the Romesco dip on the side and enjoy!

END NOTES

1. Patty W.Siri-Tarino, Qi Sun, Frank B.Hu, and Ronald M.Krauss, "Saturated Fatty Acids and Risk of Coronary Heart Disease: Modulation by Replacement Nutrients," Curr Atheroscler Rep. 12, no. 6 (2010): 384–390, doi: 10.1007/s11883-010-0131-6

2. Surender K Arora and Samy I McFarlane, "The case for low carbohydrate diets in diabetes management," Nutr Metab 2, no. 16 (2005), doi: 10.1186/1743-7075-2-16

3. Jeff S.Volek, Stephen D.Phinney, Cassandra E.Forsythe, Erin E.Quann, Richard J.Wood, Michael J.Puglisi, William J.Kraemer, Doug M.Bibus, Maria Luz Fernandez, Richard D.Feinman, "Carbohydrate Restriction Has a More Favorable Impact on the Metabolic Syndrome than a Low Fat Diet," Lipids 44 (2009): 297, doi: 10.1007/s11745-008-3274-2

4. Dyson, P.A., Beatty, S.and Matthews, D.R."A low-carbohydrate diet is more effective in reducing body weight than healthy eating in both diabetic and non-diabetic subjects." Diabetic Medicine 24, (2007): 1430–1435, doi: 10.1111/j.1464-5491.2007.02290.x

5. CHANGE TO: Christopher D.Gardner, PhD; Alexandre Kiazand, MD; Sofiya Alhassan, PhD; Soowon Kim, PhD; Randall S.Stafford, MD, PhD; Raymond R.Balise, PhD; Helena C.Kraemer, PhD; Abby C.King, PhD, "Comparison of the Atkins, Zone, Ornish, and LEARN Diets for Change in Weight and Related Risk Factors Among Overweight Premenopausal Women," JAMA 297, no. 9 (2007): 969-977, doi: 10.1001/jama.297.9.969

6. Gary D.Foster, Ph.D., Holly R.Wyatt, M.D., James O.Hill, Ph.D., Brian G.McGuckin, Ed.M., Carrie Brill, B.S., B.Selma Mohammed, M.D., Ph.D., Philippe O.Szapary, M.D., Daniel J.Rader, M.D., Joel S.Edman, D.Sc., and Samuel Klein, M.D., "A Randomized Trial of a Low-Carbohydrate Diet for Obesity — NEJM," N Engl J Med 348 (2003):2082-2090, doi: 10.1056/NEJMoa022207

7. JS Volek, MJ Sharman, AL Gómez, DA Judelson, MR Rubin, G Watson, B Sokmen, R Silvestre, DN French, and WJ Kraemer, "Comparison of Energy-restricted Very Low-carbohydrate and Low-fat Diets on Weight Loss and Body Composition in Overweight Men and Women," Nutr Metab 1 (2004): 13, doi: 10.1186/1743-7075-1-13

8. Y.Wady Aude, MD; Arthur S.Agatston, MD; Francisco Lopez-Jimenez, MD, MSc; Eric H.Lieberman, MD; Marie Almon, MS, RD; Melinda Hansen, ARNP; Gerardo Rojas, MD; Gervasio A.Lamas, MD; Charles H.Hennekens, MD, DrPH, "The National Cholesterol Education Program Diet vs a Diet Lower in Carbohydrates and Higher in Protein and Monounsaturated Fat," Arch Intern Med. 164, no. 19 (2004): 2141-2146, doi: 10.1001/archinte.164.19.2141.

9. Bonnie J.Brehm, Randy J.Seeley, Stephen R.Daniels, and David A.D'Alessio, "A Randomized Trial Comparing a Very Low Carbohydrate Diet and a Calorie-Restricted Low Fat Diet on Body Weight and Cardiovascular Risk Factors in Healthy Women," The Journal of Clinical Endocrinology & Metabolism 88, No 4 (2009), doi: http://dx.doi.org/10.1210/jc.2002-021480#sthash.iGAbMelf.dpuf

10. M.E.Daly, R.Paisey, R.Paisey, B.A.Millward, C.Eccles, K.Williams, S.Hammersley, K.M.MacLeod, T.J.Gale, "Short-term Effects of Severe Dietary Carbohydrate-restriction Advice in Type 2 Diabetes—a Randomized Controlled Trial," Diabetic Medicine 23, 1 (2006): 15–20, doi: 10.1111/j.1464-5491.2005.01760.x

11. Sharon M.Nickols-Richardson, PhD, RD, , Mary Dean Coleman, PhD, RD, Joanne J.Volpe, Kathy W.Hosig, PhD, MPH, RD, "Perceived Hunger Is Lower and Weight Loss Is Greater in Overweight Premenopausal Women Consuming a Low-Carbohydrate/High-Protein vs High-Carbohydrate/Low-Fat Diet," The Journal of Pediatrics 105, 9 (2005): 1433–1437, doi: http://dx.doi.org/10.1016/j.jada.2005.06.025

12. Stephen B.Sondike, MD, Nancy Copperman, MS, RD, Marc S.Jacobson, MD, "Effects Of A Low-Carbohydrate Diet On Weight Loss And Cardiovascular Risk Factor In Overweight Adolescents," The Journal of Pediatrics 142, no. 3 (2003): 253-258, doi: http://dx.doi.org/10.1067/mpd.2003.4

13. William S.Yancy Jr., MD, MHS; Maren K.Olsen, PhD; John R.Guyton, MD; Ronna P.Bakst, RD; and Eric C.Westman, MD, MHS, "A Low-Carbohydrate, Ketogenic Diet versus a Low-Fat Diet To Treat Obesity and Hyperlipidemia: A Randomized, Controlled Trial," Ann Intern Med. 140, no. 10 (2004): 769-777, doi: 10.7326/0003-4819-140-10-200405180-00006

14. Frederick F.Samaha, M.D., Nayyar Iqbal, M.D., Prakash Seshadri, M.D., Kathryn L.Chicano, C.R.N.P., Denise A.Daily, R.D., Joyce McGrory, C.R.N.P., Terrence Williams, B.S., Monica Williams, B.S., Edward J.Gracely, Ph.D., and Linda Stern, M.D., "A Low-Carbohydrate as Compared with a Low-Fat Diet in Severe Obesity, " N Engl J Med. 348 (2003):2074-2081, doi: 10.1056/NEJMoa022637

15. Grant D Brinkworth, Manny Noakes, Jonathan D Buckley, Jennifer B Keogh, and Peter M Clifton, "Long-term Effects of a Very-low-carbohydrate Weight Loss Diet Compared with an Isocaloric Low-fat Diet after 12 Mo," Am J Clin Nutr 90, no. 1 (2009): 23-32, doi: 10.3945/ajcn.2008.27326

16. H.Guldbrand, B.Dizdar, B.Bunjaku, T.Lindström, M.Bachrach-Lindström, M.Fredrikson, C.J.Östgren, F.H.Nystrom, "In Type 2 Diabetes, Randomisation to Advice to Follow a Low-carbohydrate Diet Transiently Improves Glycaemic Control Compared with Advice to Follow a Low-fat Diet Producing a Similar Weight Loss," Diabetologia 55 (2012): 2118, doi: 10.1007/s00125-012-2567-4

17. Eric C Westman, William S Yancy, Jr, John C Mavropoulos, Megan Marquart, and Jennifer R McDuffie, "The Effect of a Low-carbohydrate, Ketogenic Diet versus a Low-glycemic Index Diet on Glycemic Control in Type 2 Diabetes Mellitus," Nutr Metab 5 (2008): 36, doi: 10.1186/1743-7075-5-36

18. Yancy WS Jr, Westman EC, McDuffie JR, Grambow SC, Jeffreys AS, Bolton J, Chalecki A, Oddone EZ, "A randomized trial of a low-carbohydrate diet vs orlistat plus a low-fat diet for weight loss," Arch Intern Med. 170, no. 2 (2010: 136-45, doi: 10.1001/archinternmed.2009.492

19. Reddy PH, "Mitochondrial oxidative damage in aging and Alzheimer's disease: implications for mitochondrially targeted antioxidant therapeutics," J Biomed Biotechnol. 3 (2006): 31372, doi: 10.1155/JBB/2006/31372

20. Stuart G.Jarrett, Julie B.Milder, Li-Ping Liang and Manisha Patel, "The ketogenic diet increases mitochondria glutathione levels," Journal of Neurochemistry 106, no. 3 (2008): 1044–1051, doi: 10.1111/j.1471-4159.2008.05460.x

21. CHANGE TO: Sullivan PG1, Rippy NA, Dorenbos K, Concepcion RC, Agarwal AK, Rho JM., "The ketogenic diet increases mitochondrial uncoupling protein levels and activity," Ann Neurol. 55, no. 4 (2004): 576-580, doi: 10.1002/ana.20062

22. William Davis MD, "Wheat and its head-to-toe destruction of health," *Wheat Belly: Lose the Wheat, Lose the Weight, and Find Your Path Back to Health* (Pennsylvania: Rodale, 2014): 106.

23. "Insulin Resistance and Prediabetes," National Diabetes Information Clearinghouse, last modified June 2014, https://www.niddk.nih.gov/health-information/health-topics/Diabetes/insulin-resistance-prediabetes/Pages/index.aspx.

24. Jeremy M. Berg, John L. Tymoczko, and Lubert Stryer, "Glucose Can Be Synthesized from Noncarbohydrate Precursors," in *Biochemistry*, 5th ed. (New York: W. H. Freeman, 2002).

25. Rajiv Chowdhury, MD, PhD; Samantha Warnakula, MPhil; Setor Kunutsor, MD, MSt; Francesca Crowe, PhD; Heather A.Ward, PhD; Laura Johnson, PhD; Oscar H.Franco, MD, PhD; Adam S.Butterworth, PhD; Nita G.Forouhi, MRCP, PhD; Simon G.Thompson, FMedSci; Kay-Tee Khaw, FMedSci; Dariush Mozaffarian, MD, DrPH; John Danesh, FRCP; and Emanuele Di Angelantonio, MD, PhD, "Association of Dietary, Circulating, and Supplement Fatty Acids With Coronary Risk: A Systematic Review and Meta-analysis," Ann Intern Med.160, no. 6 (2014): 398-406, doi: 10.7326/M13-1788

26. Siri-Tarino PW, Sun Q, Hu FB, Krauss RM, "Meta-analysis of Prospective Cohort Studies Evaluating the Association of Saturated Fat with Cardiovascular Disease," Am J Clin Nutr. 91, no. 3 (2010): 535-546, doi: 10.3945/ajcn.2009.27725.

27. "Prevalence of Overweight, Obesity, and Extreme Obesity Among Adults: United States, 1960–1962 Through 2011–2012," Centers for Disease Control and Prevention, last modified September 2014, http://www.cdc.gov/nchs/data/hestat/obesity_adult_11_12/obesity_adult_11_12.htm#table2.

28. "Dietary Recommendations and How They Have Changed Over Time," Agriculture Information Bulletin no. (AIB-750) 494 pp, U.S.Department of Agriculture (1999): 36-44, URL: http://www.ers.usda.gov//media/91022/aib750b_1_.pdf.

29. "The Food Guide Pyramid," U.S. Department of Agriculture (1992): 2-11, URL: http://www.cnpp.usda.gov/sites/default/files/archived_projects/FGPPamphlet.pdf

30. "Preventing Diabetes," Centers for Disease Control and Prevention, last modified September 2015, http://www.cdc.gov/diabetes/basics/prevention.html

31. Swasti Tiwari, Shahla Riazi, and Carolyn A.Ecelbarger, "Insulin's Impact on Renal Sodium Transport and Blood Pressure in Health, Obesity, and Diabetes," American Journal of Physiology 293, no. 4 (2007): 974–984, doi: 10.1152/ajprenal.00149.2007

INDEX